The Ultimate Weapon

Philip F. Lawler

REGNERY GATEWAY • CHICAGO

Published by Regnery Gateway, Inc.
360 West Superior Street
Chicago, Illinois 60610

Manufactured in the United States of America

Library of Congress Cataloging in Publication Data

Lawler, Philip F.
  The ultimate weapon.

  1. Catholic Church. National Conference of Catholic
Bishops. Challenge of peace. 2. Atomic warfare—
Religous aspects—Catholic Church. 3. Peace—Religious
aspects—Catholic Church. 4. Catholic Church—United
States—Pastoral letters and charges. 5. Catholic Church
—Doctrines. 6. United States—Military policy—Religious
aspects. I. Title.
BX1795.A85C39   1983 Suppl.5   261.8'73   84–42696
ISBN 0-89526-826-4 (pbk.)

For Leila

*When one finds a worthy wife, her value is far
  beyond pearls.*
*Her husband, entrusting his heart to her, has an
  unfailing prize.*
*She brings him good, and not evil, all the days of
  his life.*

—Proverbs 31:10–12

CONTENTS

Introduction

The bishops have spoken. With the promulgation of their massive pastoral letter, "The Challenge of Peace: God's Promise and Our Response," the Roman Catholic bishops of the United States have ended a process that lasted nearly three years, and brought down an unprecedented amount of public scrutiny on the hierarchy. But if the Catholic Church in this country is to respond—if the bishops are to be successful in their efforts to make this a "peace church"—then the publication of the pastoral letter must be only the first step. Now the issue must be taken into every diocese, and every parish, and translated into the popular understanding that will build a real grass-roots campaign to ease the dangers of nuclear war.

So today, all around the United States, large and small groups of Catholics are discussing the bishops' letter in particular, and the morality of nuclear defenses in general. And the question is not of interest merely to Catholics. If the nation's 50 million Catholic citizens are aroused, the political effects will touch all Americans, indeed all the people of the Western world. One prominent Church official has begun reminding skeptical reporters that the United States has more Catholic parishes than local Post Offices. Now, if the Church leadership has its way, every one of those parishes will devote some time and attention to discussing the dangers of nuclear war.

What, exactly, are those dangers? Do they threaten our lives, or our souls? And how can we respond? By changing our minds or our votes? By designing new military strategies, or by conceding that no military strategy is adequate in a nuclear age? By giving up the arms race, or redirecting it? By marching in demonstrations? Or by penance and prayer?

In their Pastoral Letter, "The Challenge of Peace: God's Promise and Our Response," the bishops have attempted to answer those questions and others. But the bishops certainly did not end the discussion. On the contrary, as they themselves noted, "This pastoral letter is more an invitation to continue the new appraisal of war and peace than a final synthesis of the results of such an appraisal." In the "implementation" of the bishops' message, those crucial questions must be argued afresh, and the answers interpreted, until the stance of the Catholic Church is clear not only to the millions of Catholic laymen in the United States, but also to their fellow citizens.

This book is written as a contribution to that discussion—an effort to help define and interpret the Catholic approach to nuclear strategy. More specifically, it is written to help Catholic Americans understand the bishops' letter and the issues that surround it. Although I hope this will be useful to anyone puzzled by the moral dilemmas of modern warfare, I am particularly hopeful that it will be useful to individuals, parishes, and dioceses as they wrestle with the bishops' Pastoral Letter.

Let me make one point clear at the outset. I do *not* think that the bishops were wrong to involve themselves in the discussion of national defense. *Nor* do I think that their Pastoral Letter itself was wrong, in its basic thrust or in its fundamental conclusions. To be sure, I do think that the bishops have given short shrift to some ticklish problems, and I question some of their technical judgments. More to the point, I have serious reservations about the manner in which the bishops' debate was conducted. Worst of all, I believe that the Pastoral Letter sadly neglects the power of prayer, the most important Catholic response to the danger of war. I have made no effort to conceal these criticisms.

Different readers will find themselves most interested in different aspects of the Pastoral Letter. The bishops have tried to address a very wide audience, and in the process have produced a delicately balanced document. "The Challenge of Peace" was crafted carefully, in the hope that faithful Catholics, secular politicians, popular journalists, and leaders of other religious communities all could gain something from it. As a result, every reader is likely to find some passages in the Pastoral Letter more relevant than others. Journalists might ignore all the Scriptural references. Politicians might leap immediately into the discussion of particular defense policies. Some readers will find the document too distinctively Catholic; others will say its Catholic perspective is not strong enough.

In the course of this short book, I do not directly address the question of *why* the bishops sought out such a broad audience. But that is a question worth asking. During my several years of work as an editor,

I incessantly told writers to keep their primary audience clearly in mind. Reading "The Challenge of Peace" with an editor's critical eye, I suspect that the bishops sacrificed some of their impact on their primary audience—faithful American Catholics—in order to avoid distracting the secular audience, which had never before shown much interest in their pastoral work.

Nevertheless, I can still insist that the bishops' Pastoral Letter constitutes a valuable contribution to our discussion of national defense. It comes at a time when the United States desperately needs to re-examine its defense policies, and it helps clarify the real moral issues we face. "The Challenge of Peace" is, for the most part, a balanced statement of the Catholic position on a terribly important and complex issue.

We Americans are preoccupied with political arguments; we often forget that political issues can be seen quite clearly from other perspectives. For the bishops to issue a Pastoral Letter giving not the Democratic view, nor the Republican view, but the *Catholic* view of national defense comes as a healthy shock; it is something quite new, and therefore thought-provoking. Through my own involvement in the discussion and debate that preceded the bishops' final vote on the Pastoral Letter, I can attest to the fact that many of the participants in that debate developed, refined, and even changed their own ideas under the influence of the bishops' work. Even those who disagreed violently with the thrust of the Pastoral Letter were forced to think through their opposition, and restate it in clear, cogent terms. Thanks in large part to the bishops' work, many Americans today have reconsidered their own ideas about national defense, and realized the moral hazards that come attached to any nuclear arsenal.

In the constant struggle of partisan politics, the debate over national defense strategy can disintegrate into a rigid ideological battle, with each side ignoring the valid claims of the other. That is unfortunate; it could be deadly. Those who worry about the dangers of nuclear war cannot be dismissed simply as cowards, or dupes of Communist propaganda; their concerns are natural and authentic. On the other hand, those who insist on the need to defend against Soviet threats are not war-mongers; they are upholding a vital moral imperative. The bishops' Pastoral Letter, properly understood, should break down some of the partisan political postures that inhibit proper discussion of our dilemma.

Here I must stress that, if it is to be useful, the bishops' work must be properly understood. By that I mean that the Pastoral Letter must not be seen simply as an attack against the nuclear strategy of the Reagan Administration. If the bishops have done nothing more than issue a partisan political broadside, there is no reason to pay attention to their statement. Alas, most of the press coverage has emphasized exactly that aspect of the controversy. Occasionally, the temptation to read the Pastoral Letter as a mere campaign document has overwhelmed many interpreters, including even a few of the bishops themselves.

The worst possible result that the bishops' letter could generate would occur if this politically charged interpretation reigned supreme. "The Challenge of Peace" is an invitation to re-think our national defense policies, and see if there might be rational alternatives to our present situation. The bishops have taken the first step toward a new national consensus on defense strategy—a step that should be welcomed by virtually all parties, since virtually all parties agree that our current situation is unsatisfactory. So it would be a shame if the Pastoral Letter became one more political football, to be tossed back and forth angrily by the two major contending factions.

At the risk of gross oversimplification, I would characterize those two factions as politically liberal and conservative. The liberal faction, in this very rough division, tends toward suspicion of American military strength, and sees the best hope for peace in some form of American initiatives toward disarmament. The conservative faction emphasizes the military threat posed by the Soviet Union, and trusts in a strong American defense posture to preserve the peace by deterring Soviet aggression.

This book is written from a perspective much more sympathetic toward the latter, conservative approach to American defense. While I cannot always agree with my conservative friends, I do find their arguments more convincing than those of their ideological opposites. And I find, to my dismay, that the liberal faction has enjoyed a near-monopoly on the interpretation of the bishops' work.

The views and ideas put forth in this book are not typical of the reaction to the bishops' statement. While I can endorse the Pastoral Letter itself, I cannot endorse the prevailing interpretation of that letter—an interpretation which is put forward, all too often, by people who are unfamiliar with the Catholic tradition of discussion and debate on war and peace. As American Catholics begin considering the effects of that Pastoral Letter, and pondering their own responses, they should be aware of the many different, legitimate responses that faithful Catholics can make to follow the bishops' lead. The bishops have called Catholics to work for peace. How can anyone reject that call? And as for *how,* exactly, we should work for peace—that subject calls for a great deal of careful reflection. The views presented in this book offer a counterbalance, an alternative to the views most often heard by those who answer the bishops' call.

The bishops' Pastoral Letter offers a uniquely valuable perspective on the debate about nuclear defenses. But it also affords a great potential for mischief and demagoguery. It is quite possible to brandish the Pastoral Letter in one hand, while the other hand puts forward a set of partisan political ideas that are unsupported—or actually contradicted —by the contents of that Letter. Anyone aiming for partisan political gains can invoke the bishops' arguments, and claim their support. Then, if his political prejudice is challenged, he can backpedal comfortably, pointing out that of course his purpose—like that of the bishops—is nonpartisan. In other words, he can cloak a partisan argument in the mantle of religious respectability.

Even honest, conscientious people can succumb to this temptation, wrapping their own beliefs in the bishops' message without bothering to make their audience aware of the distinction between a document of the hierarchy and a personal prejudice. This sort of presentation makes demagoguery easy; disagreement with the interpreter becomes tantamount to rejection of the Gospel. Indeed, one serious indictment that I bring against the bishops stems from my belief that they aided and abetted the demagogic interpretation of their work. Consciously or unconsciously, the bishops encouraged those who parlayed the Pastoral Letter into political advantage.

So, again, I have written this book in an effort to partially offset the unfair advantage that a certain political perspective has gained through the use and abuse of the bishops' work. Inevitably, some readers will characterize my work as a "loyal opposition" to the bishops, and think that they are thereby flattering me. They are not. I am not setting myself up in opposition to the bishops. I *am* opposing the misuse of the bishops' extraordinary Pastoral Letter. Toward that end, this book emphasizes one undervalued perspective. This is not a "balanced" approach; nor is the accompanying list of recommended readings a "balanced" list. But my readers will have no trouble finding representatives of the opposite viewpoint in Catholic bookstores, secular and diocesan newspapers, and the products of their own local Church groups. This book will have served its purpose if it makes some readers realize that the bishops' letter is not a simple document, nor a call to blinkered partisanship, but a plea for much more serious thinking on a terribly complicated moral issue.

"The Challenge of Peace" covers many different aspects of the study of war and peace. Some sections of the Pastoral Letter—such as the long section devoted to Scriptural exegesis—are outside the scope of this book. I hope that no reader will infer that I consider those sections less important. On the contrary; if someone asked which single section of the Pastoral he should read, I would unhesitatingly recommend the Scriptural analysis. The Word of God has a power far greater than any human ideas, and yields far more valuable insights.

In writing this book, however, I have concentrated

on the questions that directly concern faithful Catholic laymen: the direct practical implications of the bishops' initiative. The bishops have given us their guidance; it remains for the laity to translate that guidance into practical political work.

Unfortunately, not many people will read "The Challenge of Peace." Whatever its merits might be, the Pastoral Letter is much, much too long. So thousands of Catholics will take their instruction not directly from the bishops, but from the teachers, pastors, and journalists who interpret the letter for them—even from secular newspapers and television reports. That is unfortunate; no interpretation can be as accurate as the primary text. To help remedy this weakness, I have incorporated the bishops' official précis of their letter as Appendix A. This précis contains all of the crucial features of "The Challenge of Peace," and none of the prejudices of outside interpreters.

For some other students, the bulky pastoral letter will be no problem; some people will find themselves swept up by the controversy, and look for more background information. For those readers, I have also provided a list of further readings on the crucial questions of war and peace. These recommended readings, like this book as a whole, represent points of view too often neglected by Catholic activists. Anyone genuinely concerned with the entire question of war and peace, and the Catholic tradition pertaining to it, should become familiar with these views as well as those more commonly found in the available literature. In a nuclear age, national defense is a terribly complex subject. There are many one-sided arguments, but no one-sided solutions.

For over a generation now, we have been mired in the Cold War. Young Americans like myself, born after the end of World War II, know nothing else. We have grown accustomed to thinking of a world divided into opposing camps—a world in which two huge military machines stand in quiet constant confrontation. We forget, occasionally, that this is a very odd period in world history. Confrontation is not a natural condition. Ordinarily, by good means or bad, international conflicts are finally resolved.

Years of "peaceful" coexistence have dulled our senses, and tempted us to forget that our world cries out for an end to the confrontation between East and West. We ordinarily feel that there is no end in sight; the Cold War is taken as a fact of life. "The Challenge of Peace" bids us to shake off our lethargy, and consider the problem of war in a new light. The end to the Cold War is *always* in sight. It could end today, or tomorrow, with a global war of unprecedented horror. Or it could end with our tacit surrender, and the subjection of millions more to Soviet tyranny. This book argues a third possibility. The Cold War could end—not soon, perhaps, but within the span of our lives—peacefully. Yes, we could lose the Cold War peacefully. But we could also win.

I *The Controversy Unfolds*

Peace seemed far away. We children at St. Mary's School were frightened. Nikita Khrushchev, the dictator of the Soviet Union, was actually coming to visit the United States. We had already learned, in our first few years of grade school, about the malignant atheism that ruled that country. We knew about the invasion, subversion, and persecution that marked Soviet power. Now the man who guided that diabolical power was headed for our shores.

We children had no illusions about the power of evil and no doubt that Khrushchev represented that power. Now he would set foot on our country's soil; who knew what damage he would wreak? So it was a great solace to us when the nuns escorted us down to the auditorium, where, under Father Toland's leadership, we prepared to face our enemy. Nikita Khrushchev had hideous nuclear weapons at his disposal—weapons that could end our lives without warning. But young as we were, we knew how to respond. We had the ultimate weapon. To stave off whatever damage Khrushchev might intend, and to help end the Soviet threat forever, we prayed the rosary together.

That scene was set in 1959. Now, a generation later, Catholic schoolchildren are again being called into assemblies and reminded of the horrors on nuclear weapons. After a long, intense, and dramatic debate among the bishops, the Catholic Church in the United States has inaugurated a massive campaign to instruct the faithful on the problem of war.

To millions of Americans, the active posture of the Catholic Church came as a shock. Was this the same Church that had instructed grade-school children to pray the rosary for the conversion of Russia? The same Church whose pastors had thundered from the pulpits about the sins of godless Communism? Oh, yes, there had been a few isolated priests here and there who spoke out against warfare, but now the hierarchy of the Church was taking a very aggressive stance on that same issue.

The movement to "Ban the Bomb" is nearly as old as the bomb itself. As soon as the early 1950s, a group of respected American intellectuals led by Robert M. Hutchins began raising the argument that atomic weapons were so hideously destructive that nothing could justify their use. But Hutchins' campaign never attracted much of a following, least of all within the hierarchy of the Catholic Church. On the contrary. As late as the Vietnam War, the most powerful American prelate, New York's Cardinal Spellman, was an outspoken defender of our armed forces. By the time the National Conference of Catholic Bishops (NCCB) expressed reservations about the war in Vietnam, popular opposition to the war was already so widespread that the bishops' statement passed unnoticed. Few Americans would have considered the Catholic Church an active force in the discussion of international politics. But insofar as the Church did seem to take a stance, that stance was decidedly conservative.

Then—it seemed quite suddenly—the Church appeared on the opposite wing of the political spectrum. The NCCB had made nuclear weapons a top priority, and early discussion of that question made it clear that the prelates were leery about the government's nuclear arsenal. True, the great majority of bishops still remained fairly discreet. But those who did speak out were not contradicted. And the outspoken bishops were making more and more dramatic statements.

As the momentum of the bishops' peace movement began to build, each successive action brought new media attention, adding to the public perception that an enormous change was taking place. Dozens of bishops lent their support to the campaign for a nuclear freeze. (Eventually, a majority of the U.S. bishops had signed on as sponsors of at least one of the several competing freeze proposals.) Dozens more joined *Pax Christi,* an international Catholic organization with strong pacifist leanings. The national president of *Pax Christi,* Bishop Thomas Gumbleton of Detroit, was named to the committee of five bishops delegated to prepare the pastoral letter on nuclear defense.

All around the country, bishops hit the headlines with their condemnation of the arms race and of American defense policies. Bishops Sullivan (in Richmond, Virginia), Mahoney (Stockton, California), and Weakland (Milwaukee, Wisconsin) issued blunt, controversial statements. In San Francisco, Archbishop John Quinn advised Catholic hospitals not to comply with civil-defense efforts, since compliance might encourage the belief that civil defense was a realistic response to nuclear war. In Amarillo, Texas, Bishop Leroy Matthiesen urged Catholic workers to leave their jobs in a munitions factory, and volunteered to help support their families until they found other work. And in Seattle, Archbishop Raymond Hunthausen referred to a Trident submarine base as the "Auschwitz of Puget Sound," and announced that he would refuse to pay his federal taxes to support the defense budget.

Each of these statements incurred a storm of protest from angry Catholics, and a flood of letters, pro and con, to the editors of local newspapers. Catholics and non-Catholics alike registered strong reactions. Some welcomed the bishops' newfound interest in defense issues; others demanded that they stick to their own business, and stay out of politics; still others found technical flaws in the bishops' arguments, and insisted that they had gone too far, or not far enough. But above all, most Americans were simply astonished.

The outspoken messages of the activist prelates—who came to be known as the "peace bishops"—resurrected a nagging question about Catholics as citizens of the United States. From the time when the first waves of Irish and German Catholic emigrants arrived in this country, there had been a persistent anti-Catholic sentiment, fired by (among other things) the widespread belief that all Catholics owed their first loyalty to Rome, rather than to their home country. Millions of Americans looked upon their Catholic neighbors as potentially unpatriotic, or perhaps even actively subversive.

Very, very gradually, the suspicion of Catholic

citizens dwindled. Anti-Catholicism remained in many other guises, to be sure, but few Americans actually worried about whether Catholics would switch sides in a crucial national conflict. The threat of "rum, Romanism, and rebellion" had never materialized. The Church in America had supported the institutions of the country, and its government, steadfastly. Bishops had exhorted their flocks toward good citizenship, and any fears of subversion had long since dissolved. Catholics had fought bravely through several American wars, and the 1960 election of John Kennedy had signaled the death of formal anti-Catholicism as a political force.

But now a new question was being raised. Now the bishops of the Catholic Church were leading the charge against nuclear weaponry—against the mainstay of U.S. military defense. So naturally non-Catholics began to wonder once again: in the pinch, would Catholics in military service refuse to obey orders? Would the nation suddenly realize that some 25% of its citizens had opted out of the Cold War struggle?

Certainly a few bishops were hinting at just such a conclusion. In Texas, Bishop Matthiesen had counseled the people of his diocese to quit working in defense plants. And in Seattle, Archbishop Hunthausen delivered a rousing call for tax resistance:

We have to refuse to give incense—in our day, tax dollars—to our nuclear idol. On April 15 we can vote for unilateral disarmament with our lives. Form 1040 is the place where the Pentagon enters all our lives, and asks our unthinking cooperation with the idol of nuclear destruction. I think the teaching of Jesus tells us to render to a nuclear-armed Caesar what that Caesar deserves—tax resistance.

Once again, American citizens were astounded. But in fairness to the "peace bishops," they should not have been. The bishops' interest in defense was not particularly new, nor was their skepticism about nuclear weapons a sudden development. The Catholic Church has a long, distinguished tradition of interest in matters of war and peace, and a body of thought—the "just-war" tradition—that has developed over literally hundreds of years. As modern weapons have increased the horrors of war, Catholic leaders have progressively tightened the conditions that governments must meet before they can justify warfare. Earlier in the 20th century, Pope Pius XII declared that offensive warfare could no longer be condoned; the devastation wreaked by modern war had grown out of proportion to the any political goals that offensive warfare might fulfill. Only self-defense, or the defense of other nations against unjust aggression, could be used as a justification for war.

In the aftermath of World War II, Pius XII issued still more cautions about atomic bombs. It was he—the most unabashed anti-Communist to occupy the Chair of Peter, and the first Pope of the nuclear era—who first condemned the arms race, and called for the elimination of nuclear arms. Each of his successors in turn embraced the same position: the arms race is immoral, and must be stopped; nuclear weapons should be eliminated from the world altogether. During the Second Vatican Council, the world's bishops underlined the traditional Catholic teaching that condemned the intentional killing of innocent civilians, and referred pointedly to the dangers of "modern weapons of mass destruction" as violating that stricture. The Vatican Council called for "a whole new approach" to the evaluation of war and the pursuit of peace.

Within the United States, the official posture of the Catholic Church had been developing gradually for several years. In 1976, the American bishops repeated yet again that it would be immoral to make civilians the targets for nuclear strikes—a direct, unmistakable condemnation against bombing population centers in the Soviet Union. In "To Live in Christ Jesus," the bishops also pointed out that if the action itself would be morally wrong, then it would be morally wrong to *intend* or to *plan* such an action. Thus, the bishops made it clear that nuclear warfare would be morally objectionable, and implicitly questioned whether even a policy of nuclear deterrence could be justified. In 1979, in testimony to a U.S. Senate committee considering the SALT II arms-control agreements (which the NCCB strongly supported), the influential Cardinal Krol of Philadelphia warned that the Catholic Church could condone nuclear deterrence only so long as there was active progress being made toward eventual disarmament.

Meanwhile, as the American prelates defined their attitude toward nuclear weaponry, the Church faced increasing public criticism for its role in another political question: abortion. The bishops condemned the 1973 Supreme Court decision that had made abortion on demand legal, and called for a halt to the slaughter. Pope John Paul II, during his 1978 trip to the United States, stood in the shadow of the Washington Monument to deliver a stinging condemnation of abortion. In nearby Arlington, Virginia, Bishop Welch regularly joined picket lines outside abortion clinics. And in 1980, Archbishop Joseph Bernardin of Cincinnati registered his outrage when the Democratic Party platform effectively endorsed abortion. Each of these initiatives drew intense criticism from a hostile press.

Stung by Archbishop Bernardin's criticisms, President Jimmy Carter demanded—and received—an audience with him and with other leaders of the Catholic hierarchy. The statements issued after that meeting sought to soften the impact of Archbishop Bernardin's comment by pointing out that abortion was only one among a number of issues to be considered in appraising the major parties' platforms. In fact, as the campaign developed, it became clear that many bishops were more comfortable, on balance, with the Democratic platform than with the Republican alternative. After Ronald Reagan's election, Church activists became regular critics of the new Administration: on economic affairs, on tactics in dealing with Central America, on welfare policy, and above all on strategic defense.

The bishops' drive to produce a pastoral letter on national defense began with a decision at the annual meeting of the NCCB in November, 1980. In the spring of 1981, Archbishop Bernardin was named to chair a committee of five bishops that would produce a draft of the pastoral letter to be amended and/or approved at the NCCB meeting scheduled for November 1982. Two other members of that committee attracted a great deal of public notice during the ensuing debate. Bishop Gumbleton, the leader of *Pax Christi,* became the leader of the "liberal" effort to condemn nuclear weapons. Bishop John O'Connor, whose duties as military vicar gave him pastoral responsibility for Catholics in the armed forces, emerged as the chief spokesman for the "conservative" forces. Bishops Daniel Reilly (of Norwich, Connecticut) and George Fulcher (of Lafayette, Indiana) completed the committee's membership. These last two were the "quiet men" on the committee, virtually ignored by the major media despite the overwhelming publicity that attended every utterance by Bishops Bernardin, O'Connor, and Gumbleton.

The committee began its work in July 1981 with a meeting in Washington, and immediately the criticism began. As a special technical consultant, the Bernardin Committee chose Bruce Russett, a Yale political scientist who, despite an impressive string of publications on international affairs, was not known principally as an expert on nuclear strategy. Conservative critics wondered aloud how the committee could have overlooked William O'Brien, a professor at nearby Georgetown University who has been studying the just-war tradition for over twenty years, and is widely recognized as the leading authority in the field. As it turned out, O'Brien was just one of the many witnesses who appeared before the committee to be heard and interviewed. At each of several meetings during the first stage of their work, the committee members called in several experts to give testimony in their fields of expertise: Scriptural scholars and nuclear strategists, theologians and government officials. In its loosely structured but methodical way, the committee heard each expert's testimony quickly, then moved along. After many such fact-finding meetings, and hours of discussion, the committee issued its first draft of the pastoral letter in July 1982.

The first draft was sent to all the American bishops, all the committee's consultants, and a number of other interested parties. It was marked as "confidential" and—remarkably—it did not leak widely to the press. But rumors about its contents were plentiful.

Many newspapers reported that the bishops had condemned nuclear weapons—a report vague enough to be credible, and yet dramatic in its implications. No popular report contained the text of the draft itself, and many reports failed to mention that it was *only* a draft. Nevertheless, as sketchy and misleading as the reports were, they were the first widespread public acknowledgement of the bishops' efforts. From that point forward, each new development in the pastoral letter was greeted by headlines, editorials, and debates in the mass media.

In comparison with the three subsequent versions of the pastoral letter, the first draft was by far the shortest (about 60 typewritten pages) and the most radical in its theological and political analysis. Among those few people who *did* read the text, reactions were widely mixed, according to the readers' political and theological leanings. Liberal activists were delighted and encouraged; their glowing reports fueled the newspaper accounts of the bishops' aggressive intentions. Conservatives, on the other hand, were horrified. Just as the first draft ensured that the subsequent debate would attract intense media attention, so too it ensured that the issue would be highly, bitterly politicized. The bishops were no longer speaking in purely theological terms, to be obeyed or ignored according to one's religious beliefs. They were touching on one of the most controversial political issues of the day, at a time when that issue was becoming increasingly controversial in its own right. The bishops were becoming political actors, and they would suffer—or enjoy—the partisan debate accordingly.

After pondering reactions to the first draft, the bishops' committee made their second draft public in October 1982. If they had been aiming for the maximum public impact, their timing could not have been better. It was the height of the campaign season for off-year Congressional races, and the nuclear freeze was the most controversial issue on the public agenda. After weeks of rumors and speculation, the media finally had a full text to analyze. In fact, in their anxiety to supply information to the media, NCCB staffers apparently neglected their primary responsibilities. The Reagan Administration officials responsible for following the bishops' progress first learned about the new draft in the pages of the *New York Times*. One official consultant to the bishops' drafting committee was forced to borrow a copy of the new text from a colleague. Many newspapers carried detailed accounts of the draft before the local bishops had had a chance to digest it. Again, liberals were pleased with the contents of the draft, and conservatives displeased. As the date of the bishops' November meeting approached, public interest reached new heights.

By now, there could be no mistaking the direction of the bishops' movement, and a conservative reaction began to form. William Clark, National Security Adviser to President Reagan, wrote a detailed critique of the draft, challenging its factual assumptions about U.S. strategic policies. Returning the NCCB's snub in kind, the Administration made the Clark letter available to the press immediately; it was Archbishop Bernardin's turn to learn about this development by reading the *New York Times* account. An *ad hoc* coalition of conservative Catholic laymen* announced their disagreement with the bishops' strategic analysis, and scheduled a press conference to coincide with the beginning of the November NCCB

*The coalition was chaired by the author of this book.

meeting. Bishops around the country began receiving an avalanche of mail, and editorial writers devoted reams of paper to congratulating, questioning, or condemning the bishops' statement. Another *ad hoc* group, composed of 24 prominent Americans (not all Catholics), announced their support for the bishops' position. In all the furor, one simple, crucial fact was almost entirely ignored. The bishops' statement was still just a draft; no official announcement had been made.

The contents of the second draft were certainly controversial. But for many observers—especially conservatives—the procedures of the bishops' committee were now even more controversial. Why were the bishops extending themselves to the technical questions of nuclear weapons? Was it coincidence that brought out a dramatic draft statement at the height of a Congressional campaign? Why was the NCCB staff so avidly courting the mass media? Writing in a new publication put out by concerned Catholic laymen, *Catholicism in Crisis,* Kerry Koller accused the bishops of making a highly politicized independent newspaper, the *National Catholic Reporter,* their paper of record. But, Koller continued, that was only a minor problem:

> . . . but what is *really* wrong with the document lies on an entirely different, and much deeper, level. Simply put, it is this: the total lack of discussion of these issues within the context of the Catholic tradition of political thought. The Catholic tradition was born of the labors of countless thinkers throughout two millenia of human history. It is one of the pillars of the Western democratic tradition. It is the frame-

work of all recent social papal and conciliar decrees. It is entirely absent here.

In raising that point, Koller illustrated another intriguing element in the growing controversy. By and large, the Catholics who most violently objected to the bishops' activism on nuclear defense were extremely supportive of their prelates' involvement in the controversy over abortion. By the same token, many of the Church activists who welcomed the bishops' attempt to assert their authority on this question were ordinarily averse to *any* assertion of ecclesiastical authority.

This argument—the argument over the nature of ecclesiastical authority, as opposed to the companion argument over the bishops' practical conclusions— pointed in turn to a longstanding disagreement among American Catholics. For years, liberal Catholics had shown an inclination to mistrust their bishops, advancing the argument that the Catholic laity should be free to make its own moral choices. When Pope Paul VI issued his encyclical *Humanae Vitae,* reaffirming the traditional Catholic ban on artificial means of birth control, that resistance to episcopal authority assumed massive proportions. Theologians openly advised Catholic laymen to ignore their bishops, and do whatever they themselves thought best. Now many of the same theologians were counseling a recalcitrant laity to *accept* the bishops' authority. Conversely, many of the Catholics who had most adamantly supported the bishops' authority on the question of contraception drew the line on national defense. So the pastoral letter threatened to aggravate another internal problem that vexed the American Church. If the bishops took a radical stance, would the laity respond? Or would the last vestiges of episcopal authority be cast in doubt, so that American Catholics were confirmed in practicing selective obedience to their pastors?

In view of the burgeoning controversy, Archbishop Bernardin (who in the interim had been promoted to head the diocese of Chicago, America's largest Catholic diocese), announced that the bishops probably would not meet their anticipated schedule; he would counsel against a final vote at the November meeting. Instead, the bishops would discuss the strengths and weaknesses of the second draft in November, the drafting committee would make the necessary revisions, and a third, final draft would be prepared for a vote at a special NCCB meeting in May 1983. That recommendation was quickly adopted.

Still, when the bishops arrived in Washington for the November meeting, the level of public interest was phenomenal. Ordinarily, newspapers mention the bishops' annual meeting briefly, in the rear pages, if at all; television news programs ignore the meeting completely. But on this occasion, cameras followed the bishops everywhere. Reporters crowded into the meeting room, and hustled to briefings to learn about arguments that they had previously ignored. Every major newspaper, radio, or television outlet featured the bishops' argument, and virtually every one reported that the bishops had taken a clear stand against nuclear weaponry. Radio and television reporters competed for interviews with the principal actors: Archbishops John Roach (the president of the NCCB) and Bernardin, Bishops Gumbleton and O'Connor, and the staff director of the NCCB committee, Father J. Bryan Hehir.

Particularly in the eyes of conservative critics,

Father Hehir began to assume a central role in the public discussion. A popular rumor claimed that he was the author of the second draft. He and the bishops on the drafting committee denied that rumor, but the same reports continued to spread. Undeniably, Father Hehir was a major influence on the committee, particularly in the creation of that second draft; the arguments in that text closely follow arguments he had put forth in his own personal writing on the subject. But Father Hehir also furnished a convenient target for those who preferred not to believe that the bishops realized what they were doing—that the American prelates were dupes of a staff effort to usurp their authority. A short, thin, intense man with bushy eyebrows and a rapid-fire speaking style, Father Hehir was a perfect object for conspiracy theorists. Throughout the public discussion, photographers obliged this fascination by producing innumerable pictures of Father Hehir leaning over to whisper into the ear of Archbishop Bernardin: a portrait (for those who chose to see it that way) of episcopal innocence traduced.

As the November meeting progressed, the media reports stressed the bishops' clear consensus favoring the thrust of the pastoral letter. But most reporters, having no background in the special arts of Church politics, missed some vital signals that indicated the need for changes in the second draft. A number of bishops made personal "interventions" arguing for specific changes in the arguments of the letter. In an informal poll, 71 bishops—more than enough to block the passage of the letter by the required two-thirds majority—indicated strong reservations, and 12 found "basic disagreements" with the arguments of the draft. Perhaps most important of all, but least noticed by the popular press, was a statement by

Archbishop Pio Laghi, the Vatican's representative to the United States. For anyone who was paying attention, Archbishop Laghi's words constituted a clear, authoritative caution to the American hierarchy:

> It is safe to say that you will encounter criticism. . . . Hence the prudence of the decision to defer final publication of the Pastoral Letter. . . . For when the time does come for you to speak, it is important that you speak with clarity and greatest possible unanimity. . . . Perhaps the need for clarity and unanimity will lead to less specific teaching than some would wish.

Naturally, those comments from the Papal Delegate were not the first indication that the Vatican was interested in the work of the American bishops. Nor was it the last. In January 1983, Archbishop Bernardin was summoned twice to Rome. One summons seemed to suggest Vatican worries about his committee's work; he was called, along with Archbishop Roach and Father Hehir, to a "consultation" with a number of European bishops to discuss the moral arguments of the pastoral letter. (The results of that consultation are discussed in Chapter Two.) But the other summons seemed to constitute a strong vote of confidence: Pope John Paul elevated Archbishop Bernardin to the rank of Cardinal, making him a Prince of the Church. In response to reporters' queries, the Cardinal-designate averred that, indeed, his elevation indicated the Vatican's pleasure with the committee's work. That analysis was extraordinarily unusual—prelates do not often discuss the reasons for their appointment—and probably misleading— the archbishop of Chicago is traditionally given a cardinal's red hat, reflecting the importance of his huge pastoral bailiwick. But it is true that Archbishop Bernardin's promotion came in near-record time. Certainly it is reasonable to say that the Pope's action was a gesture of confidence in Cardinal Bernardin, and in his ability to bring the committee's work to a successful conclusion.

(The popular press, usually so indifferent to promotions within the American hierarchy, devoted an unusual amount of attention to the Vatican's reasons for promoting Cardinal Bernardin. Just a few months later, however, the media ignored another appointment that suggested another Vatican message. Almost immediately after the bishops' final decision to endorse the Pastoral Letter, Bishop John O'Connor was also promoted—from his post as an auxiliary bishop serving under the lead of New York's Cardinal Terence Cooke, to a diocese of his own in Scranton, Pennsylvania. If it was fair to say that the Vatican had expressed its confidence in Cardinal Bernardin, the chief moving force behind the Pastoral Letter, it was also fair to notice the Vatican vote of confidence in Bishop O'Connor, the most influential "conservative" force in the drafting process. As usual, the signals from Rome were not easy for outsiders to fathom, and reporters interpreted them at their own risk.)

After weeks of relative quiet, the Bernardin committee issued a third draft in April 1983. Careful observers should have been able to predict the changes that this third draft embodied, yet many reporters were nonetheless surprised. Following the suggestions of the bishops' November discussions, and the comments made by the other European bishops at the Vatican consultation, the committee had moderated the draft in both tone and content. While still clear in its condemnation of nuclear warfare, and skeptical about the justification for a policy of deterrence, the third draft was not nearly as dramatic as either of its predecessors. And in an extremely significant change that many careless readers overlooked, the third draft also took great pains to distinguish between the authoritative teaching of the Catholic Church and the particular strategic judgments of the American bishops.

Now it was the liberals' turn to express disappointment. Newspaper accounts suggested (and Cardinal Bernardin hotly denied) that the bishops had buckled under to the pressure of the Reagan Administration. In the *National Catholic Reporter,* Jesuit Peter Henriot worried that the new draft was too hostile in its comments about the Soviet Union. Gordon Zahn, an antiwar activist of long standing, wrote in the *National Catholic Register:* "Confronted with pressure from concerned policy makers, the drumfire of criticism from the Catholic right, and the exaggerated caution of European bishops (and the Holy See?), the bishops' committee 'blinked.'"

The political implications of the third draft were, to be sure, less damaging to the Reagan Administration than those of the first two drafts. But the most significant changes were not political but theological. In the third draft, the bishops' committee paid much more careful attention to their role as religious leaders in defining public morality. And they accentuated, beyond question, the importance of the traditional Catholic "just-war" teachings. Some observers found this theological emphasis distressing in itself. The editor of the *National Catholic Reporter,* Arthur Jones, dismissed the third draft as "religious-sounding mush."

Once again, the stage was set for a dramatic confrontation when the bishops assembled in May, in

Chicago, to render a final decision on their pastoral letter. But now it was the liberal wing of the Catholic Church that felt the need to regroup and muster its forces. When the bishops arrived at the Palmer House hotel on May 1, they would find demonstrators in the lobby, on the streets, and outside their meeting rooms—demonstrators chanting slogans, carrying placards, and calling for the bishops to reaffirm their commitment to nuclear disarmament.

The most important change that the Bernardin committee made between the second and third drafts was an effort to clarify the authority of the proposed pastoral letter. At the outset, the third draft pointed out that bishops are moral leaders rather than strategic analysts, and their judgment on technical issues is not binding on the Christian conscience. So different sections of the pastoral letter were assigned different levels of authority. When they reaffirmed the traditional teachings of the universal Church, the bishops invoked their full authority as teachers and rulers. When they made their technical judgments, they called for a respectful hearing, but admitted that their judgments were fallible.

Unfortunately, in the eyes of the popular press the bishops' technical judgments were the *only* important facet of the debate. From the moment when the second draft made its appearance on the headlines, reporters had stressed the bishops' judgments on issues such as the MX missile, limited or tactical nuclear warfare, and above all the nuclear freeze. Blinded by this exclusively secular, political perspective, most reporters thought that the most significant change between the second and third drafts involved only one word. In the second draft, the text called for a "halt" to the arms race; the media interpreted this as a vote for the nuclear freeze. The third draft called for a "curb" on the arms race, and the pundits somehow decided this change was a vital success for the Reagan Administration, signalling the bishops' unwillingness to endorse the freeze outright.

So, as the bishops arrived in Chicago, the secular press buzzed with speculation about whether the NCCB as a whole would accept "curb" instead of "halt" in the final pastoral letter. The resulting spectacle was almost humorous; a group of nearly 300 prelates worried about the comparative connotations of two similar words, while an equal number of reporters (who would ordinarily sneer at theological hair-splitting) egged them on with incessant questions on exactly that topic. The debate on that single-word change was intense. Since these two innocent words had become so highly charged with partisan political significance, Archbishop Szoka of Detroit suggested that the bishops reject both options, and call for the arms race to "cease"; since the press had not yet analyzed that word, it could not be seen as a victory for either liberals or conservatives. But the bishops would not duck the issue. After extensive debate, they opted for a different sort of compromise. The word "halt" would be re-inserted into the final text, but a footnote would warn against interpreting the text as favoring any single political proposal.

The footnote failed to register with the public. The press had been poised to declare a victory for either the Reagan Administration or the nuclear-freeze movement, according to the final choice of word. In fact, the footnote even failed to convince the bishops themselves. Asked by a reporter whether the vote could be taken as an endorsement of the nuclear freeze movement, NCCB president Archbishop Roach replied, "That's right. That's absolutely right."

Hundreds of media accounts that evening reported that the bishops had decided their posture "on the nuclear freeze." Within a week after the bishops' vote, two other national organizations had embraced the freeze explicitly, citing the bishops' lead. The mass media had come to Chicago proclaiming the importance of the single word—halt or curb—and when that vote was taken, the media leaped immediately to their conclusion: the bishops had discarded the conservatism of the third draft, and reinstated the liberalism of the second. All on the basis of one word.

As usual, the media missed the more important debates which were to follow. Soon after the bally-hooed vote to "curb" the arms race, the bishops plunged into a series of resolutions that restored much of the second-draft language regarding practical strategic judgments. Led by Archbishop Quinn, the bishops voted to toughen their rejection of limited nuclear war, first use of nuclear weapons in warfare, and targeting of civilian population centers. After several such votes, a pattern was established. The bishops were inclined to take an aggressive stance on strategic questions, especially now that they had made it clear that such judgments were not infallible; they wanted to emphasize their rejection of nuclear warfare in the strongest possible terms. Only one, Archbishop Philip Hannan of New Orleans, consist-ently opposed each new change in the wording of strategic judgments. After each session, the doughty Archbishop Hannan was surrounded by curious re-porters. But during the debate, he carried the stan-dard by himself. "I didn't expect to be so alone," he confessed afterward.

While Archbishop Hannan claimed that the NCCB majority was making *incorrect* strategic judgments, several other bishops wondered aloud why they were making any strategic judgments at all. Bishop O'Connor, the most conservative voice on the Bernardin committee, made the case most clearly. After a career in the military chaplaincy, he said, and years of studying military tactics and ethics, and after all the technical debates of the drafting committee, he *still* felt incompetent to judge the technical merits of different strategic options. Why then should the NCCB attempt such difficult judgments?

To that argument, Washington's influential Archbishop James Hickey offered the prevailing response. Yes, he admitted, the bishops' technical judgments might be unsophisticated. But to avoid such judgments would be an admission that "we would have labored in vain" in producing the pastoral letter. So the technical judgments came fast and furious, with the more liberal interpretation consistently winning approval.

Eventually, however, the bishops finished their discussion of military strategy, and moved onto the more familiar ground of ethics and theology. (More familiar, that is, to the bishops; the secular media apparently missed the importance of these arguments entirely.) Now the tide turned, and the cautious approach of the third draft was reaffirmed. Cardinal Bernardin used all his persuasive powers to forestall a movement to condemn the morality of nuclear deterrence outright. The bishops clarified their contention that while pacifism is a legitimate moral option for individuals, the just-war tradition remains the focal point of Catholic teaching; they reminded pacifists of their obligation to help somehow in the defense against unjust aggressors.

Then, as a hectic meeting roared toward its conclusion, there came another set of votes that should have raised the eyebrows of anyone familiar with recent

Church history. A generation ago, Catholic bishops would never have risked the political venture that the NCCB had now irrevocably endorsed. But the bishops of that earlier generation felt no inhibitions when Church rules and regulations were concerned. Sunday Mass, meatless Fridays, Lenten and Eucharistic fasts—all those rules were enforced unblinkingly. The bishops gathered in Chicago felt precisely the opposite about their authority: they welcomed a chance to air their political preferences, but refused to risk their authority to assert traditional Church authority. So the bishops strongly recommended a return to meatless Fridays as a form of penance on behalf of peace, but they voted against making that abstinence mandatory. They agreed that Catholics should pray the rosary for peace, but refused to make any such suggestion in the text of their letter.

As the bishops discussed those recommendations, an intriguing set of arguments appeared. One bishop worried that the laity might ignore a call for Friday fasting, since Friday is (he said) now considered a part of the weekend, when laymen cannot be bothered with further obligations. Another prelate cited St. Paul as his authority, and argued that the mature Christian conscience should not be hampered by rules and regulations. Yet another questioned whether bishops should tell laymen how to think (on questions other than nuclear strategy, apparently). From the viewpoint of the American bishops, a call for fasting, or for praying the rosary, would be *more* controversial than their call for a halt to the arms race!

Finally, after an exhausting two-day meeting, the bishops voted 238–9 in favor of the pastoral letter they had created.

The immediate public reaction to the final text was

not as heated as the reaction to either the second or the third draft. Liberals were mildly pleased, but less so than at their high-water mark of the second draft. Conservatives were displeased with the last-minute revisions, but reassured by the calmer tone that remained from their favorite third draft. The bishops had defined the issues more clearly with each successive draft, and the final document did not polarize Catholics as earlier efforts had.

Still, the reaction was considerable. The *New York Times* surprised its readers by dismissing the bishops' efforts, remarking that "There's no place to hide, even in morality." That cavalier editorial treatment produced a storm of letters from readers who supported either the bishops or the *Times* editorial writers. (Among those writing letters were former President Nixon and the bishops' chief technical adviser, Bruce Russett.) Ironically, all these letters appeared before the final text of the bishops' letter was available. Once again, public reaction preceded public understanding of the bishops' work.

Other readers expressed more cynical reactions. In *Catholicism in Crisis,* a pseudonymous editorial began, "Why else do we have bishops if not to chide Christians for lion-baiting in the Coliseum?" And columnist Patrick Buchanan quoted Eugene McCarthy as saying that whereas once the bishops received their authority "direct from the Holy Ghost, now we get it by voice vote."

The echoes of the Chicago meeting were still subsiding when the bishops began their next debate. Arriving home from the meeting, Archbishop Quinn told a San Francisco audience that the pastoral letter was a clear condemnation of nuclear warfare. As he explained it, a faithful Catholic would be obliged to disobey any order to use nuclear weapons. "No commander in chief or any human authority," he continued, "can justifiably force someone to do something that is morally wrong." Immediately, Bishop Leo Maher of San Diego took issue with Archbishop Quinn's interpretation. "There is nothing in the pastoral that says the individual is not ever permitted to use nuclear weapons," he pointed out.

While the two California prelates argued over the message of the Pastoral Letter, one angry bishop took a still more radical stance. From New Orleans, Archbishop Hannan announced that he would tell the people of his diocese to ignore the Pastoral altogether.

Who was interpreting the bishops' work better, Archbishop Quinn or Bishop Maher? Was Archbishop Hannan's non-cooperation legitimate? Did all American Catholics now share a new obligation to follow the bishops' lead? What, exactly, did the bishops say in "The Challenge of Peace"? Were their words binding for all Catholics? Before answering those questions, one must understand the crucial debates that formed the pastoral letter.

II *Questions In Dispute*

Traditionally, American Catholics vote Democratic. Catholic immigrant groups brought their political skills to this country, and used them to help set up many of the big-city political machines that formed the working base of the Democratic party for years. Catholics are equally prominent among the ethnic groups (Irish, Italian, Polish, German) and blue-collar labor unions that have formed the backbone of Democratic voting majorities. But in recent years, political analysts have sensed a change: a breakdown in the old political coalitions. After the 1980 elections, pollsters announced that the newly elected President Reagan had drawn unusually solid support among Catholic voters.

For any perceptive observers, that result was not a surprise. As a group, Catholics have enjoyed great success in this country; they understand the pocket-book issues—inflation, government spending, taxation—that Ronald Reagan emphasized. Single, emotional issues such as abortion and feminism also strike to the heart of the Catholic voting bloc; no amount of episcopal backing and filling could erase the impact of Cardinal Bernardin's lament about the pro-abortion Democratic platform. And every available survey indicates that American Catholics hold strong views on national defense: views that match the themes of the 1980 Reagan campaign.

So it was no surprise that the Reagan Administration appointed a number of Catholics to influential positions, especially in the realm of national defense. Secretary of State Alexander Haig was a practicing Catholic (whose brother is a Jesuit priest), as was National Security Adviser Richard Allen. When Allen resigned, his place was taken by another devout Catholic, William Clark. The Secretary of the Navy, John Lehman, came from one of Philadelphia's most prominent Catholic families. The Chief of Naval Operations, Admiral Watkins, and the head of the Army's Defense Nuclear Agency, General Griffiths, were only two of the many prominent Catholics in top military posts. And Ambassador Edward Rowny, the top U.S. negotiator in START disarmament talks, was yet another faithful Catholic layman.

Still, when the bishops' discussion of nuclear weapons began to assume serious political importance, the Reagan Administration seemed unprepared. Apparently, there were no active lines of communication between the White House and the offices of the U.S. Catholic Conference a few blocks away. When the U.S.C.C. wrote to the Administration, asking for a chance to talk with defense officials about the forthcoming Pastoral Letter, the request was unanswered. Then, weeks later, officials in a *different* government agency fired off a letter to the bishops, demanding to know why no Reagan officials had been invited.

Eventually that breakdown in communications was repaired, and a small delegation of powerful officials testified before the bishops' drafting committee. But the absence of regular communications between the two groups continued to show. The bishops and the Reagan officials eyed each other across a wide ideological gulf; each seemed to regard the other as an avowed political adversary.

For months, the Reagan Administration committed one blunder after another in its dealings with the bishops. White House officials ignored the bishops' drafting committee, then responded suddenly and intemperately to newspaper reports rather than analyzing the texts of the bishops' draft letters. When the Administration did make a public statement, that statement usually harped on the same themes: the power of the Soviet Union; the need to match the Soviet arms build-up step for step; the *realpolitick* dictum that strength must meet strength. If they really hoped to influence the bishops, the Administration officials could not have chosen worse arguments. By emphasizing the hard-headed issues, they reinforced the perception—widespread particularly among the "peace bishops"—that the White House simply did not recognize the moral hazards of nuclear weaponry.

Of course, not everyone in the Administration was equally inept. Secretary of the Navy John Lehman took the bishops' arguments seriously, and responded in the pages of the *Wall Street Journal* with a brilliant analysis of the moral issues involved. Admiral Watkins and General Griffiths delivered thoughtful speeches on the moral issues as well. But for the most part, the Administration preferred to abandon the moral argument, and attempted to dismiss the bishops' arguments as idealistic.

Yet the White House never abandoned the field altogether. Despairing of the possibility that they could influence the American hierarchy, Administration officials still hoped (correctly, as it turned out) that they could find some allies in the Vatican. Ambassador Rowny visited with the Vatican Secretary of State, Cardinal Casaroli, to express the government's concern. And Ambassador Vernon Walters was sent to confer with the Pope. No one can be sure how much those visits accomplished. But when the Pope delivered his thoughts on disarmament to the United Nations, the speech included a very specific affirmation that nuclear deterrence was not immoral under present circumstances.

When the Reagan Administration did actually address the merits of the bishops' arguments, the results were fascinating. The first direct controversy arose when William Clark wrote to Clare Boothe Luce, complaining about the first draft of the Pastoral. In that letter (which was eventually relayed to the bishops), Clark pointed out that the draft called for serious negotiations toward arms reduction, and yet ignored the dramatic proposals President Reagan had recently made toward exactly that goal. When the second draft again failed to mention those initiatives, Clark wrote a long letter to Archbishop Bernardin, detailing the arms-control plans that the White House had suggested, and the negotiations that were already in progress. But his arguments were in vain. The final document would only refer grudgingly to "serious efforts" that were underway, without naming those efforts. And that same sentence in the Pastoral Letter ended with the charge that "the results have been far too limited and partial. . . ."

Clark was not alone in pointing out the American efforts to slow the arms race. At the instigation of

Congressman Henry Hyde, 24 Catholic members of
Congress wrote to the now-Cardinal Bernardin, asking the bishops to reflect on—among other things—
the Soviet unwillingness to negotiate meaningful
arms limitations. In a careful response, Cardinal
Bernardin cautioned that Soviet threats should not
deflect attention from the moral questions that *American* leaders faced. But he did not mention the history
of American arms-control efforts.

A casual reader might have thought that the bishops neglected the history of arms-control efforts
because they did not want to be bogged down in the
discussion of details. But when they wrote about
weapons systems, the bishops were not at all loath to
provide details. In the second draft, the bishops
argued fiercely against the development of weapons
that might seem designed for first-strike use, and
mentioned the MX missile in that category. In the
final version, the MX missile is not mentioned in
the text, but a footnote refers to both the MX
and the Pershing missile as suspect.

Immediately after mentioning the MX missile, the
second draft made a blanket statement condemning
"The willingness to foster strategic planning which
seeks a nuclear war-fighting capability." That sentence prompted a storm of reaction from defense
officials. If our forces are not capable of fighting a
war, critics asked, how can they be useful to deter
aggressors? A deterrent force that cannot fight is no
deterrent at all. The bishops relented—a bit. In the
final text, a few words were added to soften that
crucial sentence, so that it condemned "The willingness to foster strategic planning which seeks a nuclear
war-fighting capability *that goes beyond the limited
function of deterrence outlined in this letter.*" (Italics
added to mark off new wording.)

Similarly, in both the second draft and the final Pastoral Letter, the bishops denounced: "proposals which have the effect of lowering the nuclear threshold and blurring the difference between nuclear and conventional weapons." Again the reaction was intense. Did the bishops mean to say that nuclear weapons should *not* be made less destructive? John Lehman argued in the *Wall Street Journal* that:

> The bishops' opposition . . . is absurd in terms of the basic argument. One cannot complain about the immorality of nuclear war because of its unlimited impact and then oppose the development of a strategy or a technology that seeks to limit its impact.

While the argument swirled around these strategic judgments, an even hotter dispute involved a matter that seemed to be simply an issue of fact. The bishops, in their early drafts, had condemned plans to bomb enemy civilian centers. In a letter to the bishops' staff director, Father Hehir, Eugene Rostow, then the head of the Arms Control and Disarmament Agency, pointed out that "it is United States policy that civilians are not proper objects of an attack." Judge Clark emphasized the same message in his letter to Archbishop Bernardin. If the bishops believed that the U.S. strategic plans involved nuclear strikes against population centers, they were wrong. To underscore the point, the Secretary of Defense took a dramatic step. In his annual report to Congress on the U.S. defense posture, Caspar Weinberger used language that he had lifted directly from the bishops' draft: "Under no circumstances may such weapons be used deliberately for the purpose of destroying civilian populations."

Once again, the bishops refused to back down. True, they admitted, the official strategic plans might not call for attacks against civilians. But were there not 60 military targets located within the city of Moscow alone? Since the Soviet government locates most of its military installations in or near cities, any nuclear strike would probably involve hideous levels of civilian casualties.

Still, that was not quite the same point. The likelihood of civilian casualties would certainly figure in the moral analysis when strategic targets are chosen—especially when those civilian casualties would be so heavy. But since the casualties would not be intended, and since the military necessity to target Soviet war-making machinery is demonstrable, the moral issue would still be difficult to judge. If the threat to civilians is *direct,* however, the Catholic tradition is unmistakably clear: direct attacks against civilians are unreservedly condemned. In short, if the threat against civilians is unintended, then U.S. strategic policies might be morally justified; if the threat is intentional, the Catholic Church must condemn U.S. policy without qualification.

Clearly, the stakes in this disagreement were extremely high. And although the question seemed to be straightforward enough, neither the bishops nor the White House could devise a statement that satisfied the other's worries. So theologian German Grisez suggested a compromise solution; the Pastoral could leave the question open, and simply call attention to the traditional Catholic teaching. Grisez suggested a carefully worded sentence: "If the present U.S. nuclear deterrent is focussed on noncombatants and its threat includes a choice to kill them if deterrence fails, then that deterrent is immoral and nothing can justify it." The bishops did not respond.

Ironically, the targeting of noncombatants *had,* in the past, been a feature of U.S. strategic policy. But as Defense Secretary Weinberger made clear in a letter to the bishops, the Reagan Administration had adapted its strategic policies to stop targeting cities. In other words, the bishops had arrived on the scene too late to invoke the most powerful argument of the just-war tradition. Here was an opportunity for the bishops to cooperate with the Administration, urging the government on toward a more moral defense strategy. When the bishops met in Washington in November 1982, Bishop Edward O'Rourke of Peoria recommended: "that in our pastoral we vigorously protest against the relatively few warheads which are still aimed at cities as being inherently unacceptable." But that recommendation, too, was ignored.

One last, vital question completed the list of points in dispute: Can a nuclear war be limited? The bishops doubted that any nuclear weapon could be used without leading to the use of *all* nuclear weapons; they feared that even a single use of one tactical nuclear warhead in battle would escalate into an all-out exchange, and the demise of our civilization. For that reason, the bishops inveighed against the new generation of nuclear weapons, such as the neutron warhead, which are designed for battlefield use in strictly limited conditions. The weapons themselves might not inflict the same massive destruction as a larger nuclear warhead, the bishops pointed out, but they might nonetheless lead an enemy to use those larger warheads. Once the nuclear threshold has been breached, there might be no way to stop short of a global holocaust.

So the bishops frowned on tactical nuclear weapons, and on any plans to make limited nuclear war possible. But their argument was based entirely on the premise that nuclear war could not be controlled. If escalation is inevitable, then the risks of using tactical nuclear weapons become unacceptable, and the moral basis of the U.S. defense posture is destroyed. But if escalation is *not* inevitable—if a limited nuclear war is in fact possible—then our deterrent posture is morally sound. In fact, if a limited nuclear war is possible, then by the bishops' own logic, the U.S. should develop a whole new range of tactical nuclear weapons—an approach exactly opposite the one suggested by "The Challenge of Peace."

Fully recognizing how central the question of escalation was to their entire argument, the bishops took a strong stand, proclaiming themselves convinced "of the overwhelming probability that major nuclear exchange would have no limits." Conceivably, the Pastoral Letter admitted, a smaller, limited use of nuclear weapons might not lead to escalation. But the bishops implied a tremendous distinction between a nuclear weapon—no matter how small— and a conventional weapon—no matter how large:

> The debate should include the psychological and political significance of crossing the boundary from the conventional to the nuclear arena in any form. . . . To cross this divide is to enter a world where we have no experience of control, much testimony against its possibility and therefore no moral justification for submitting the human community to this risk.

On this point, the Reagan Administration could only offer indirect rebuttals. Obviously, no one can be sure whether limited nuclear war is possible— until it happens. Consequently, no one could assure the bishops that escalation was impossible. Reagan aides could only ask why the bishops were so sure of their own argument. The bishops' second draft had cited several defense analysts to support their conclusion, but none of the quotations came from officials on the Reagan team. In a footnote, the draft quoted a 1979 report by former Defense Secretary Harold Brown, who admitted that it was "not at all clear" that nuclear war could be controlled. But that footnote omitted the following paragraph of Brown's report, in which he speaks about the possibility of working toward controllability. And several of the quotations cited in the draft referred to major nuclear exchanges, rather than battlefield uses of tactical nuclear devices. On a pivotal point, the White House argued, the bishops were showing a weak grasp of technical details.

All the Administration's arguments accomplished nothing. When the final text appeared, the Pastoral Letter made the same points even more forcefully. The question of escalation was a question of faith, and the bishops could not believe in the possibility of limited nuclear war. "When it comes to controllability," Father Hehir told one audience, "the bishops are agnostic, bordering on atheism."

After months of confused bickering between the White House and the N.C.C.B., the debate reached a typically ludicrous conclusion when the bishops' drafting committee released its third draft of the Pastoral Letter. White House spokesmen applauded the new draft, and implied that the bishops had now endorsed Administration policy. In response, Cardinal Bernardin and Archbishop Roach fired off a press release, announced that they "could not accept any suggestion that there are relatively few and insignificant differences between U.S. policies and the policies advocated in the pastoral." That exchange took place early in April—almost a full month before *any* Pastoral Letter had been approved!

White House officials were not the only ones who disagreed with the Pastoral Letter on technical questions. Just before the American bishops met in Chicago to ratify "The Challenge of Peace," the Catholic bishops of West Germany released a statement of their own which endorsed the strategic policy of "flexible response"—a policy that includes preparation for tactical nuclear warfare. Did that mean that a nuclear strike could be used in response to a conventional attack? The head of the German episcopal conference responded, "I do not dare to say no."

At the same time, some politicians were interested in issues beyond the bishops' technical recommendations. In their letter to Cardinal Bernardin, Henry Hyde and his fellow Catholic Congressmen stressed a glaring theological error in the second draft:

> In all the burgeoning literature of apocalypse surrounding this issue we have never encountered such a startling statement as the second draft contains, when it says: "Today the destructive potential of the nuclear powers threatens the sovereignty of God over the world He has brought into being." The notion that mere creatures could do anything to "threaten the sovereignty of God over the world" strikes us as one definition of Original Sin.

Congressman Hyde won his point; that sentence was stricken from the final text.

When the American bishops argued with the Reagan Administration over technical judgments, the bishops won. But when the dispute involved theological principles, the American bishops faced the full weight of the Vatican, and the results were very different.

No one could say that today's Vatican is "hawkish" on questions of war and peace. Pope John Paul II has repeatedly condemned the arms race, and called for disarmament in a series of emotionally charged speeches. His principal deputy, Cardinal Casaroli, has been known for years as one of the Church's leading advocates of *rapprochement* with the Soviet empire. The Pope had repeatedly encouraged the American bishops in their study of nuclear morality. So when the leaders of the National Conference of Catholic Bishops were called to Rome for consultation, the discussion did not revolve around political differences. The Vatican was concerned with fundamental religious principles. And on those principles Rome would not compromise.

After the Rome consultation, both the Vatican and the American bishops released bland statements, affirming their basic agreement on the need to study the moral issues raised by modern weaponry. The Pope's support for the Pastoral Letter was again emphasized, and the American bishops announced that they did not expect to make many changes in their third draft. But behind that facade of unity there were several serious disagreements. And when a summary of the consultation (prepared for distribution to all the American bishops, at the request of the Vatican) eventually leaked to the press, it became clear that the Roman officials had not minced words.

The first vital question on the docket in Rome was the American bishops' point of entry into the strategic debate. No one present denied the importance of the moral issue, and no one suggested that bishops should stay out of politics. Rather, the Vatican sought assurance that the Pastoral Letter would emphasize fundamental moral principles, rather than concentrating too heavily on the "contingent judgments" that could be left up to the individual Catholic conscience.

That point reflected a time-tested understanding about the nature of a Catholic bishop's authority. The bishops, as defenders of Catholic orthodoxy, have the final authority on questions of principle. Individual Catholics, on the other hand, must decide questions of prudence for themselves. That is, the bishops devise the general rules for moral behavior, but the individual, who alone knows all the factors that affect his particular situation, must put those rules into practice in his own life. (For example: the bishops tell married Catholics to avoid adultery; they do not say—because they cannot know—whether a particular married man should avoid spending time alone with a particular married woman. Only those individuals know whether or not they are behaving prudently.) Thus, the bishops might enjoin Catholics to work toward peace, but each Catholic must decide for himself how he can advance the cause of peace most effectively.

The Vatican officials wondered whether the American bishops were moving outside their realm in the Pastoral Letter. Why had the American bishops based so many judgments on debatable technical arguments? Should those technical arguments have been left in the hands of the laity? Would those strategic judgments deflect attention from the more important moral principles?

Beyond that, the Vatican officials worried about how well the Pastoral Letter stated some fundamental moral principles. Many readers had interpreted the second draft of the Pastoral Letter as saying that although nuclear deterrence was immoral, it could be justified temporarily because it prevented greater evils. This, orthodox Catholic scholars pointed out, was a form of moral reasoning known as *consequentialism*—the belief that the morality of an action can be judged by its consequences. And consequentialism has been condemned repeatedly by the Catholic Church.

According to Catholic theology, an individual can never intentionally undertake an immoral action, regardless of the consequences that action might bring. The end does not justify the means. To be sure, one should always carefully appraise the likely consequences of any moral act, and at times the consequences will have a bearing on the final moral judgment. But if the action is inherently immoral, then no amount of second-guessing can justify it.

As it happens, the consequentialist theory has played a prominent role in recent American theological disputes. During the debate over the morality of artificial contraception, several prominent American theologians argued that the "beneficial" results of contraception were sufficient to justify interference with the natural process of reproduction. Then and now, the Vatican disagreed. And it was no surprise that Germain Grisez, a distinguished defender of the Church teaching on birth control, became an outspoken critic of the Pastoral Letter. (Interestingly enough, Grisez argued that nuclear deterrence can *only* be justified by consequentialist logic; he hoped for a clear-cut episcopal condemnation of U.S. defense policies.)

By the time the American bishops assembled in Chicago in May 1983, the consequentialist position had been thoroughly defeated. The drafting committee had made crucial changes in the wording of the third draft, eliminating any vestiges of that sort of reasoning. Professor Grisez, who had been horrified by the second draft, found no consequentialist flaws in the third. During the bishops' final debate, Cardinal Bernardin dismissed one suggested amendment simply by saying that it might seem to endorse a consequentialist position.

The Vatican was similarly successful in rooting out a second theological deficiency. In the first and second drafts, the bishops had appeared to say that pacifist examples were on a par with the just-war tradition as official teachings of the Catholic Church. Not so, the Vatican consultants insisted. Nor were the American bishops on solid ground when they said that early Christians had been pacifists. One may or may not accept pacifism, but one cannot say that the Church has endorsed it alongside the just-war tradition. In unusually candid language, the Vatican group labelled the Pastoral Letter "factually incorrect" in its treatment of this issue.

Pacifism, in the Catholic tradition, is indeed one legitimate approach to the problem of war. But only an individual can legitimately choose the pacifist option; a state has the responsibility to protect its citizens. In fact, an individual who does choose pacifism must not forsake the people who depend on him for protection. Celibate priests and the religious could certainly abstain from war; that is the reason why ministers are exempt from military service to this day. But laymen cannot justify pacifism so readily; the duty toward defense is compelling.

Advocates of Christian pacifism can invoke the story of Jesus Himself, refusing to defend Himself in front of Pontius Pilate. Throughout the history of the Church, other great saints have made the same decision to accept injustice rather than to fight. That heroic pacifism, however, has an indispensable moral element. Jesus died to save our souls. Martyrs died—and continue to die, even today—because they see their deaths as a means of impressing people with the power of the faith. The essence of Christian pacifism is the willingness to die for Christ.

As a plan for an entire nation, pacifism therefore encounters two overwhelming obstacles. First is the question of a nation's responsibility to its citizens and its allies. It is one thing for an individual to sacrifice his own life; it is quite another for a nation's leader to sacrifice the lives of his people. And if a great power such as the United States laid down its arms, what would befall the millions of people all around the globe who look to the U.S. for protection? Second is the question of a nation's spiritual state. An individual can offer his life to the Lord as a sacrifice, knowing how readily Jesus enfolds martyrs in His arms. But a nation is composed of many people—some prepared to meet their Maker, some not. Martyrdom does not save a nation's soul.

Early drafts of the Pastoral Letter also failed to make an important distinction between pacifism and non-violence—a distinction that our popular literature rarely observes. Men like Gandhi and Martin Luther King, so often invoked as exemplars of pacifism, were actually exponents of non-violent resistance. A true pacifist does not resist government power, no matter how unjust the government may be. An exponent of non-violence, on the other hand, resists an unjust regime with every tool at his disposal *except* armed force. The tools of non-violent resistance: strikes, demonstrations, civil disobedience, tax resistance, even sabotage—all can wreak havoc on a regime.

Even today, non-violent defense might be an appropriate option for a small nation. Faced with a threat from a much stronger country, the small nation could simply send out the word that, in the event of an invasion, the entire country would grind to a halt. Trains would not run; telephones would not be answered; stores would be closed. Perhaps the aggressor would be dissuaded; perhaps he would decide that the small country was not worth conquering.

For an international power, however, non-violence faces the same obstacles as pacifism. First, it offers no help to allies. Second, it presumes a great deal of courage from the citizenry; it presumes that thousands—perhaps millions—of ordinary people will make great sacrifices, and resist the pressure of the conquering army. Non-violence is a realistic option for a group that is united by a strong spiritual commitment. Poland's Solidarity movement is such a group. America, wracked with so many different sorts of dissension, is not.

The pacificism prevalent in the West today is a far cry from the pacificism of the early Christians, who chose martyrdom rather than fight for Caesar's idolatrous regime. The few genuine advocates of non-violent resistance preach to a small, idealistic audience. Today, the great bulk of popular anti-war rhetoric is based explicitly on simple, selfish fear. Shortly after being elevated to his post by Pope John Paul II, Cardinal Lustiger of Paris, a survivor of the Nazi concentration camps in World War II, expressed his contempt for American pacifism. It was, he said, the pacifism of people who know—or think they know—that nothing will happen to them anyway.

When the bishops' final document appeared, the references to pacifism were toned down substantially, and the just-war teachings were clearly portrayed as representing the official Catholic stance on war and peace. The third draft had answered most of the questions raised in Rome. But the American bishops assembled in Chicago amended the Pastoral Letter still further, underscoring the moral hazards of pacifism and reminding all Catholics that they must honor their duty to defend against unjust aggression.

In Rome, the American bishops faced one last, fundamental question: the nature of the bishops' authority. Did the National Conference of Catholic Bishops have any moral authority to issue binding statements? That question was raised by a formidable figure, Cardinal Joseph Ratzinger, the prefect of the Sacred Congregation for the Doctrine of the Faith— the Pope's top panel charged with guarding Catholic orthodoxy. Cardinal Ratzinger proceeded to answer his own question.

Faithful Catholics, Cardinal Ratzinger pointed out, are obliged to obey the teachings of the Pope, and of the bishop who presides over their own diocese (unless that bishop defies the Pope). But a national conference of bishops has no special status as an ecclesiastical group. An individual Catholic layman should respond to his pastor, his bishop, and the Pope; there are no other rungs on the hierarchical ladder. So the NCCB lacked a *mandatum docendi*—a license to teach. The Pastoral Letter, therefore, was not binding for American Catholics.

Even if the bishops *could* issue binding statements, Cardinal Ratzinger reiterated the distinction between judgments of principle and of prudence. The Pastoral Letter advanced a number of specific strategic solutions, alongside some immutable moral laws. As they left the Vatican consultation, the American bishops were instructed to clarify the moral authority of their Pastoral Letter, so that readers would understand which sections reflected Catholic truths and which reflected the fallible judgments of amateur defense analysts.

The third draft of the Pastoral Letter did indeed refer to the different levels of moral authority. But the question of authority continued to nag. If the bishops were not speaking as official teachers of the Catholic Church, then what was the nature of their message? Why should the laity listen? And when? If the American Catholic Church frowned on the "flexible response" defense policy, why did the German Church support it? Could Catholic teachings differ from one country to the next? Those questions were never fully answered.

In Chicago, as the final debate over the Pastoral Letter neared its completion, Archbishop Oscar Lipscomb of Nashville lamented that no one seemed very clear on this crucial question. He recommended a ten-minute suspension of the debate so that the question could be resolved. Several bishops agreed with him; none disagreed. Yet when the vote came, it was a clear rejection of his proposal to suspend debate. Yes, the most crucial question was left in a muddle. No, the bishops did not wish to discuss it.

III *War And The Christian Conscience*

War is not hell. Hell is hell. War is bad enough in itself; it needs no exaggeration.

Warfare has always been a unique horror and plague on the human condition. Today it is more frightening than ever. Innocent civilians, women and children resting in the comfort of their own homes, know that they could be killed almost instantaneously by a warhead flung across thousands of miles; they could die before they even knew a battle had begun. Nuclear weapons make it impossible to think of wars as isolated events, separate from the everyday events of life at home. In an all-out nuclear war, there is no front line, and there are no civilians. Everyone is equally vulnerable; we are all hostages, potential targets for an international terrorist campaign.

The twentieth century has changed the face of warfare, probably forever. Our weapons are more deadly than those our forefathers knew, and our ability to communicate with distant lands is immeasurably improved. We know the leaders of countries on the other side of the globe, and we have diplomatic dealings—and consequently tensions—with all of them. The earth is dotted with battle zones, and any one of those battles could mark the flashpoint for another major international conflict. No nation can be immune; every country must be aware of the potential consequences of a distant conflicts. We can span the world in less than a day, and destroy it in less than an hour.

Nuclear weapons, in short, have created a world in which everyone who reads the daily newspaper realizes that he—and everything he loves—could be destroyed before the end of that day. It is a sword of Damocles, hanging over the head of every citizen. That element—the element of fear and the urge for personal survival—is an important factor in any discussion of modern warfare. But anyone considering the moral implications of nuclear weapons must be careful not to let personal fears and dangers cloud his judgment. Fear is a powerful emotion, but not a very reliable guide to ethical judgment.

To *be* killed is, by itself, morally neutral. Every day, thousands of people die in accidents. Those deaths are unfortunate, and we work assiduously to make them less common, and yet they have no special moral significance. We humans are fallen beings. We make mistakes, and sometimes our mistakes kill us. Still, most of us live comfortably, recognizing that life is risky but going about our daily business regardless. We step into automobiles without a second thought, although we all know that traffic fatalities number in the thousands. When a friend or acquaintance is killed on the highways, we mourn for him, but we certainly do not condemn him for having died. Nor would we praise someone who, out of morbid fear of dying in a traffic accident, chose never to enter a car.

To *be* killed is morally neutral. But to *kill* is a horrible moral burden. Particularly for Christians, who believe that the Lord died to save each and every man, the crime of murder is overwhelming. For Christians, the most horrible implication of war is not that they might be killed, but that they themselves might become killers. Christianity preaches a Gospel of peace; its adherents recoil in horror at the prospect of bloodshed. Only the most severe, careful, scrupulous moral reasoning can justify warfare. Over the centuries, Christian thinkers and leaders have agonized repeatedly over that problem, and produced a very sophisticated guide to moral reasoning: the tradition of the just war.

From a Christian perspective, the loss of lives is a horrible thing, but not nearly so horrible as the loss of souls. We shall all die, sooner or later, but a lost soul is damned to an infinite, eternal punishment. Indeed, we often overlook the perils that warfare poses for the *spiritual* welfare of the warriors. Fighting brings out the worst in mankind; every war nourishes hatred and cruelty, destroys marriages and tears apart families, inculcates bitterness and cynicism and despair. Even when the cause is just, governments cannot avoid the dangers that their troops will rape and pillage. Soldiers face their death only hours after a weekend of debauchery. And all this takes place in the enervating atmosphere of everyday violence and death.

Still, if a soul is more important than a life, then it follows that a faithful Christian should be prepared to die—or even to kill—rather than to allow the loss of innocent souls. And if Jesus valued humans enough to give up His own life for us, then human dignity must be protected even at great cost. We cannot stand by quietly and watch the loss of souls, or the enslavement of peoples. We are bound, as Christians, to fight against injustice and oppression.

If the cause is just, and the battles are fought by

humane means, then warfare takes on a special moral character. The horror and sadness are unmitigated; they are always companions of warfare. But the moral horror dwindles. C. S. Lewis poses a scenario in which two courageous young men encounter each other from opposite sides of a battlefield. Each man is fully convinced that his cause is just. Each is fired by his patriotic valor and his proud determination to uphold human dignity. The two men clash, and fight, and die in each other's arms. There is an awesome dignity in that scenario—the fierce, unappreciated dignity of the warrior. Surely, there is no moral fault in the two young men; their death is a pure sacrifice for ideals—an oblation for a sinful world. We rue their death, not with tongue-clicking righteousness, but with the numb unquenchable sadness that every war brings.

In a world thoroughly stained by man's sinful nature, war is unfortunately commonplace. Christians work constantly to make war impossible, and yet they recognize that their efforts can never be wholly successful. And so while they work for peace, they do not neglect the real possibility of violence. They seek other means to resolve conflicts, but they never accede to injustice simply because violence is threatened. Pope Paul VI made the point clearly when he warned against confusing "peace with weakness (not just physical but moral), with the renunciation of genuine right and equitable justice, with the evasion of risk and sacrifice, with cowardice and supine submission to others' arrogance, and hence with acquiescence to enslavement."

When there is no other alternative save war or injustice, Christians may opt to fight. In case of self-defense, or defense of helpless third parties, the normal prohibition against killing is waived. But warfare does not mean that a Christian ceases to obey his Lord, the Prince of Peace. A Christian is always called to love his neighbor, even in time of war. He might kill, but he may not hate. He may not use the excuse of warfare to unleash savage instincts; he must maintain his prudence and his temperance even in the heat of battle. Ideally, a Christian statesman would constantly reappraise his cause, using the same scrupulous moral standards to justify each new act of violence. If at some point he determines that his cause is no longer just, or that his military goals cannot be reached without disproportionate bloodshed, then he must cease fighting immediately. Every act of war must be carefully planned to accomplish its goal with the absolute minimum of killing; every battle must serve toward a limited end, and use limited means.

As our technology has changed, so too has our attitude toward warfare. Throughout history, men have dreamed of abolishing warfare. But only in this century did world leaders begin discussing concrete plans to make that dream a reality. And as they discussed the elimination of warfare, they fought—using more and more efficient machines of destruction. International rivalries, which might once have produced a battle over a disputed border between two countries, now embroiled dozens of nations, magnifying the risks of diplomatic breakdowns. In World War I, American troops went abroad to fight the War to End All Wars. We won, but wars continued.

The campaign to end war went on, and yet warfare became more hideous than ever. World War I saw the introduction of poison gas and aerial warfare. World War II produced saturation bombing. Even while world leaders spoke about universal peace, they followed military strategies as violent and barbaric as the world has ever seen. While statesmen discussed means of restraining warfare, they placed progressively less restraint on their own forces. Alongside the concept of universal peace there grew up the concept of total war.

Of course the idea of total warfare was not a novelty—any more than the idea of world peace. General Sherman's march through Georgia illustrates how the same idea operated during the Civil War, and indeed the Old Testament abounds with stories of how victors in warfare slaughtered their rivals, their wives and children, and plowed their fields with salt. No, there is nothing new about the idea of total warfare. What is new is the widespread presumption that *all* warfare must be total warfare. Military planners would never work on that presumption, nor would leaders bent on world conquest; the concept of total warfare does not yield a productive approach to military strategy. Yet that concept exercises a special influence on American civilians—even well informed civilians—today.

The concept of total warfare replaces another older, more sophisticated understanding. The great German military theorist, von Clausewitz, referred to war as a continuation of diplomacy by other means. By that he meant that war was one more arrow in the quiver of a skillful international statesman. A nation's leader might go to war against his neighbors, but even in the heat of battle he would remember the diplomatic point he was pursuing. If he saw another way to reach his goal, he would stop the fighting immediately. War and the threat of war, according to Clausewitz and his disciples, were limited instruments to serve limited ends. A total war, with the accompanying total breakdown of diplomatic dealings, would be inconceivable.

For all practical purposes, World War II was a total war. Both the Allies and the Axis powers fought without restraint, unleashing the most powerful weapons in their arsenals. Civilians were heavily involved in the war effort; they manufactured weapons, and were the targets of enemy bombers. No effort was spared; no compromise was contemplated. Neither side contemplated a negotiated solution; the war continued until the Allies won an unconditional surrender.

Since World War II the United States has fought major wars in Korea and Vietnam. Yet somehow, those two wars are regarded as atypical. When they think of warfare, most Americans still think of World War II as the norm. When they think of war between the United States and the Soviet Union, they think of a cataclysmic event: a furious volley of thermonuclear warheads, ending in the death of our civilization: a total war. If that is the only scenario for contemporary warfare, then the pacifists are right: war can no longer be justified.

On this one point, the just-war tradition is abundantly clear. A just war is *always* a limited war. A total war, by definition, ignores the restraints that moderate the moral horror of warfare and make it ethically tolerable. Government leaders can never morally opt for the destruction of civilization. There is no such thing as a just, total war.

What, exactly, does the just-war tradition teach? To answer that question properly, one would need to spend years in painstaking research. (Appendix B lists several books by scholars who have done just that.) What follows is merely an introduction: a cursory account of a very complex, sophisticated body of thought.

Saint Augustine is generally recognized as the originator of the theory of the just war, but the fundamental premises on which that theory is based can be traced further back, to the establishment of Christianity itself. The message of the Gospels contained two stunning breaks with the ancient understanding of war and peace, life and death. First, Jesus proclaimed Himself a peacemaker, and insisted that his disciples should be the same. Of course, the peace of Christ is not the peace sought by the people of this world, as the Gospels very clearly point out. Nevertheless, the Sermon on the Mount left no doubt as to the dignity of those who work for peace here on earth. Second, Jesus emphasized with equal vigor that since His Kingdom is not of this world; the values of this world must be subordinated to those of the heavenly kingdom. Again, the Sermon on the Mount made the point clear, and thousands of Christian martyrs took the message literally. All human desires, even the desire for life itself, are trivial in the light of Christ's eternal Kingdom.

To say that Christianity is a pacifist religion, then, is to distort the faith—almost to render it trivial. A Christian leader confronts a paradox: every human life is immeasurably valuable, and yet some other things are more valuable still. Death is preferable to apostasy, or to sin. It is better to die than to be robbed of human dignity. By the same token, there are circumstances when the use of violent force may be justifiable (as in self-defense) or even obligatory (as in the defense of one's children). When these circumstances arise, the ordinary Christian preference for non-violence may evaporate.

A recurrent argument in the current debate over

nuclear weapons involves the historical fact that early Christians refused to serve in the Roman army. For the most part, it is indeed true that Christians refused to serve. But it is also true that the Roman army, during that era, expended a portion of its energy in the task of throwing Christians to the lions. And many soldiers were required to take blasphemous oaths to the Roman gods. The fact that Christians refused to serve, therefore, does not prove that they rejected military service on principle; it merely proves (in case anyone doubted it) that they considered the regime unworthy of their support.

After the conversion of Constantine, and with the gradual emergence of the Holy Roman Empire, the situation changed radically. Saint Augustine, in *The City of God,* emphasized the discrepancies between life in the sinful City of Man and in the eternal Kingdom. Nevertheless, he pointed out that the earthly kingdoms do enjoy certain authorities of their own proper sphere, and that it might be necessary to invoke civil authority and civil force to repair injustices. The power of the state is certainly not the same as the power of God, but if the state can improve man's lot here on earth, then that too is part of God's work.

From that basic understanding, the just-war theory arose, to be developed by each succeeding generation of Christian thinkers. Although a history of that development would be beyond the scope of this book, two points are worth mentioning. First, far from being pacifist, within a few centuries after Augustine, the Church was advocating holy wars: the Crusades. Second, as the march of technology brought increasing deadly power into the hands of warring nations, Christians repeatedly raised the question of whether or not warfare had become too horrible to be guided by the precepts of the just-war. With the invention of the crossbow, the cannon, the rifle, and the airplane, controversy arose that is remarkably similar to the controversy now raging over nuclear weapons. Time and again, some scholars claimed that the just-war tradition was obsolete. Time and again, they were wrong.

To say that the just-war teaching was useful, however, is not the same as to say that it was always observed. Over the centuries the Church has been no more successful in enforcing observance of its prescriptions in the realm of military theory than in its quest to rid the world of greed and lust. Wars have always been—will always be—occasions for the worst sort of atrocities. And rulers have often found ways to rationalize warfare when it suited their personal purposes. Nevertheless, one can still draw some lines, and make some moral discriminations. Surely the age of chivalry, in which (in the ideal formula) knights fought each other according to a strict code of battle ethics, was more morally advanced than our own century, with its glorification of guerilla warfare and *blitzkrieg* tactics. Nor is it a coincidence that the age of chivalry was an age of faith, when leaders were more inclined to follow the dictates of Church authorities. However much the just-war teaching might have been abused, at least in the past it was taken seriously.

Over the years, and despite the many restatements of the just-war tradition, the framework of the tradition has remained remarkably constant. A just war must conform to two sets of conditions: those that define the circumstances under which a war may permissably be waged (the *ius ad bellum* conditions), and those that define the permissable standards for the conduct of war once it is declared *(ius in bello)*.

Each of these categories is itself subdivided into individual moral tests.

Ius ad bellum describes the conditions under which a nation may override the usual precept against the taking of human life. Essentially, *ius ad bellum* demands the fulfillment of five requirements.

- First, just cause. The war must remedy or prevent a real injustice. In the past, just-war teaching also allowed punitive wars to extract vindictive justice for past transgressions. Recent statements of the tradition have discarded that interpretation.
- Second, right intention. The war must be waged for the ostensible moral purpose, not for national gain. Thus self-defense is justifiable, but imperial acquisitions are not. And once the primary goal of warfare is accomplished, the victorious nation cannot continue fighting in hope of further material advantage.
- Third, exhaustion of peaceful means. War cannot be undertaken until and unless *every* other possibility has been explored and found unavailing.
- Fourth, reasonable prospect of success. An individual might choose to fight to the death against overwhelming odds; his life is his own responsibility. But a national leader, with the lives of his subjects (and of those foreigners who might be killed in a war) in his protection, cannot require his subjects to make such a sacrifice. A war that cannot be won may not be fought.
- Fifth, competent authority. Wars must be declared and waged by a sovereign public authority, not by individual citizens or bands of outlaws.

Today's debate on the morality of nuclear warfare does not center on the *ius ad bellum* category, but concentrates instead on *ius in bello*. That focus is ironic, since modern warfare raises several very knotty questions for anyone interested in *ius ad bellum*. For instance, in an all-out nuclear war, can anyone have a reasonable prospect of success, by any plausible definition of that term? In guerilla warfare or even in an ordinary revolution, what is a sovereign authority? In an era of lightning-quick offensive weapons, what would constitute a valid declaration of war? To their credit, the bishops saw the importance of those questions and discussed them clearly. In fact, the question of whether or not a nuclear war could be considered winnable is a pivotal point in the bishops' strategic analysis.

If a nation goes to war for an unjust cause, nothing can salvage that war from moral obloquy, no matter how cautiously the battles may be waged. Even if the cause is just, the nation's leader must face the second set of moral questions: the *ius in bello* criteria.

Ius in bello can be summarized briefly in two categories.

- First, proportionality. The damage inflicted must be commensurate with the goal sought. This criterion applies to the war as a whole, and to each battlefield tactic in particular. The bishops denied that any political goal, however lofty, could justify the massive destruction of all-out nuclear war. On a tactical level, it would be unjustifiable to destroy an entire village simply to stop a single sniper.
- Second, discrimination. The conduct of war permits the killing of enemy soldiers, but not civilians. The warring party must make every effort to avoid damage to civilian and non-military targets. Terrorism is by nature indefensible; so is the

obliteration bombing that characterized World
War II.

The principles of proportionality and discrimination offer a whole host of thorny questions for
military planners facing the possibility of nuclear
warfare. For instance, if an enemy places his military
installations close to his cities (as indeed the Soviet
Union does), is it permissible to attack those installations without violating the principle of discrimination? The just-war tradition recognizes that perfect
discrimination is usually impossible; there will always
be some collateral damage to civilians. But can anything justify the awesome civilian casualties of a
nuclear detonation?

In recent years, the United States has developed
some nuclear weapons sufficiently discriminating to
destroy military targets without wreaking massive
collateral damage. In his testimony before in U.S.
Senate in 1979, Cardinal Krol allowed that "Some of
these weapons may be sufficiently discriminating so
as not to merit condemnation." But the use of even
those weapons raises another question. Is it possible
to limit the war once a nuclear weapon has been
used—however cautiously? Given the risk of escalation, is there any military objective large enough to
justify the possibility of all-out war?

Proportionality is a vital question of moral order.
Everyone agrees that military tactics should be proportionate. But proportionate to what? Before considering what sorts of weapons might be used, we
must assess the risks that confront us if *no* weapon is
used. That is, we must consider the consequences of
surrender. Suppose, for example, the Soviet Union
plunged into Western Europe in a full-scale conventional invasion. To respond with nuclear weapons

would raise *ius in bello* questions of proportionality, and *ius ad bellum* questions about beginning an unwinnable war. But to sit back and watch would be to condemn thousands of Europeans to death in conventional warfare, and thousands more to death or slavery in the "Gulag Archipelago" that would inevitably sprout up all over the continent.

These are difficult, agonizing questions. Yet before going to war, a nation's leader must answer them. In fact, they must be answered long before the war begins, because once the fighting commences a nation's options are limited. We should be preparing now to face the foreseeable dangers of warfare; the decisions that we make today will provide us with the options that we need tomorrow. There is no reason to develop a weapon that could not be used morally, nor is there any rationale for failure to develop the weapons that would be necessary for an effective, moral defense.

The just-war theory makes strenuous demands on a nation's military leaders. And that is as it should be. Christians should always welcome restraints on warfare, especially moral restraints. Properly understood, the just-war tradition is a series of reasonable but powerful moral restraints. When someone finds another guide through the moral jungle of warfare, then the just-war tradition can be discarded. Until then, what other theory can ask so many pointed questions about the potential moral hazards of nuclear warfare?

But it cannot be enough just to *ask* the tough questions about moral military strategy. The next step must be to answer those questions. So a thorough understanding of the bishops' pastoral letter and its implications requires some acquaintance with the bizarre world of nuclear strategy.

IV *A Nuclear Strategy Primer*

Si vis pacem, para bellum—if you want peace, prepare for war. Pope John Paul II quoted that old adage in his 1982 message on disarmament before the U.N. A strong national defense discourages aggressors, making peace durable.

During a time of peace, leaders have the opportunity to choose their military strategies. In the past, a warring nation occasionally managed to change its strategy in the middle of a battle, and still recover. World War II found the United States unprepared for battle, yet we managed to mobilize in time to stop the Nazi onslaught. We no longer have that margin for error. Today, when an all-out war could destroy our civilization in the space of one hour, the plans of battle must be laid out in advance. If our defense strategies are inadequate, we may never have time to improve them.

So there are two different reasons for concentrating on defense strategy today—each vitally important. First, we must avoid tempting our adversaries by our weakness; we must be strong enough to discourage potential aggression. Second, we must design a strategy today that we could use effectively tomorrow. Since our nuclear arsenal is our last line of defense, we must examine our nuclear strategy especially carefully. Is our deterrent strong enough? Do our nuclear strategies give us a plan of action that we could—or should—follow in case of war?

On one plane of understanding, the strategy of nuclear deterrence has already proven successful. For over a generation, the two great superpowers have held their conflict in check. Time and again we have come to the brink of a nuclear exchange, but we have never taken the plunge into war. For 38 years, since the bombing of Hiroshima and Nagasaki, nuclear weapons have never been used.

Or, to look at the question a bit differently, for 38 years nuclear weapons have been used every single day, always successfully. The purpose of nuclear weapons, in the eyes of American defense strategists, is to not to fight but to deter. Our nuclear forces are an integral part of our defense posture, even when—especially when—they are unused. If these fearsome weapons are ever actually used in combat, then they will already have failed. If a nuclear-tipped missile sits unused in its silo until it rots, then it has done its job perfectly. Nuclear weapons may be expensive, but the dollars sunk in the arms race are far less valuable than the lives lost in a global war.

However, we cannot afford to delude ourselves into thinking that our deterrent is working perfectly. Since the end of World War II, when nuclear weapons were used for the first (and, to date, the last) time, the world has seen hundreds of military conflicts, with thousands of casualties. As I write this chapter, open battles are raging in Lebanon, Chad, Nicaragua, Afghanistan, and Iraq; border conflicts and guerrilla struggles dot the globe. The U.S. is somehow involved in many of those conflicts, often upholding an ally against a Soviet-backed adversary. If nuclear deterrence is designed to keep the peace, it has failed.

The United States itself has been spared the trauma of invasion since the War of 1812. Occasionally, we lapse into the belief that since there are no bullets flying around us at the moment, we must be at peace. By the same token, we sometimes begin to think that since we ourselves are safe from invading forces, we need not worry about conventional war. If we could abolish the spectre of nuclear war, according to this short-sighted reasoning, we could live secure.

That logic has two glaring defects. First, although we are relatively safe from invasion now, we might not always enjoy such security. If our allies around the world fall victim to Soviet aggression, how long would the U.S. remain inviolate? Second—and more important—if we neglect the need for conventional defenses, we are neglecting our responsibility to uphold the security of our allies.

Imagine what would happen to the military balance in Europe if we dismantled the U.S. nuclear deterrent. Faced with an overpowering Soviet preponderance in conventional armaments, our allies there would have two unattractive choices: surrender or suicidal resistance. Resistance would mean hundreds of thousands of deaths, followed inevitably by submission to tyranny. And if the history of the Soviet empire is any indication, surrender would mean thousands of lives lost in the death camps that would spring up all over Europe. Perhaps we ourselves would remain unscathed—for a while—but could our consciences be quieted?

With or without a nuclear deterrent, the prospect of conventional warfare is still hideous. Conventional weapons may be less awesome than nuclear missiles, but they too can take thousands, even millions of lives. And the victim of a single bullet is no less dead than someone killed in a nuclear blast. As the casualties of conventional combat mount up, the toll can easily approach the toll of a limited nuclear war.

More to the point, the prospect of conventional war is much more immediate than that of nuclear holocaust. We hear about conventional warfare every day; and every day we hear reports of further casualties. Nuclear war is a *possibility;* conventional war is a strong *probability.* Anyone who seeks a moral approach to contemporary defense must recognize the awful calculus of warfare. If we seek to avoid slaughter, we should work first to eliminate the most likely causes of that slaughter. So when we plan our military strategies, we cannot allow the remote chance of nuclear conflict to distract us from the more immediate problem of conventional war.

An ideal defensive posture includes some protection against every conceivable threat: nuclear weapons to deter against an enemy's use of nuclear weapons, conventional weapons to counter the enemy's conventional strength. Each of these elements is important. Without a strong conventional defense, even a nuclear power cannot deter small-scale fighting; the threat of all-out nuclear war is simply not credible when it is applied to small local conflicts. No enemy would believe that a small border conflict, or a guerrilla campaign, would be met with a first-strike nuclear blast. And a strong conventional defense is not enough to ward off an adversary who possesses nuclear weapons; the nuclear power can always force surrender by threatening a nuclear strike.

In conventional warfare, deterrence is a function of military power. When an aggressive nation weighs the possibility of attacking another nation, the first consideration is the armed strength of the potential victim. If that adversary could inflict heavy losses on the aggressor, then the costs of invasion will outweigh the benefits.

In nuclear warfare, however, the workings of deterrence are somewhat more complicated. Nuclear deterrence involves not only possession of thermonuclear weapons, but also the willingness to *use* those weapons. Everyone knows that a nation will use conventional weapons to defend against an invasion. But will it use nuclear weapons, risking the total destruction of its society? Will it use those nuclear weapons—and run that risk—to defend an ally? Will a nuclear power actually destroy itself rather than surrender?

The quandary of nuclear deterrence does not yield simple solutions. It is not enough, for instance, to keep nuclear weapons in our arsenal purely as a bluff. If we have no intention of using our strategic power under any circumstances, and our adversaries realize this, then our deterrent immediately collapses. For that matter, if our adversary has any question about our willingness to respond *in extremis,* he will be sorely tempted to test our will, thereby bringing us repeatedly to the brink of nuclear holocaust. Only a firm, credible determination to use nuclear force can provide a meaningful deterrent. To bluff is not enough; we must be prepared for the worst. We must *intend* to do the very thing we so dearly hope we will *never* do.

This is the paradox of nuclear strategy: the paradox of intention in nuclear deterrence. The United States owns a huge strategic force of nuclear warheads, ready for use at any time. Our national leaders proclaim their readiness to use those warheads in defense of freedom, if necessary. The Pentagon devises scenarios for fighting a strategic nuclear war. And yet we do *not* intend to use our weapons. Or, to be more precise, the use of those weapons lies in their non-use.

So do we, or do we not, intend to use our nuclear weapons in combat? From the perspective of just-war theory, that question is absolutely crucial. If we intend to use them in battle, then we are contemplating a type of warfare that might violate the principles of proportion and discrimination. If we intend to use them solely as a deterrent, then our purposes are defensive, and therefore morally valid. But if this is our intention, we must be ready to use them. In order to defend the strategy of nuclear deterrence, we must devise a system that is neither incredible nor indiscriminate. We must be ready to deter an all-out nuclear attack by a powerful adversary, and yet we must not use immoral threats to carry out that deterrence.

In the last analysis, then, we must face the question of how we would respond to the ultimate provocation. If the Soviet Union launched an all-out attack on the United States with its full strategic nuclear might, would we respond in kind? Responding would not save any American lives; the Soviet attack would already have sealed our fate as a nation. We certainly could not *win* such a war. Should we retaliate nonetheless? To say Yes is to plan the annihilation of millions of innocent Russian civilians. To say No is to surrender before the fighting begins. There is no satisfactory solution.

Fortunately, the likelihood of an all-out Soviet attack is very slim. The leaders in the Kremlin realize that all-out war would have grim consequences for them, too. In fact, a massive strike against the U.S.

would have terrible consequences for Moscow even if we did *not* retaliate. No nation would avoid the economic fallout if American society was destroyed. The Soviet Union survives by importing American grain, and Eastern Europe needs a steady infusion of loans from New York banks. The Soviet leadership is unlikely ever to strike American soil with an all-out nuclear attack—not because they have moral scruples, but because an all-out attack would not serve their purposes.

Nevertheless, our nuclear strategy does not allow us to neglect the possibility of an all-out attack. Since we cannot guarantee our ability to stop a minor conflict from escalating into an all-out attack, we must prepare for the worst. So in the extreme position—faced with a Soviet leadership insane enough to risk a nuclear holocaust—we would be faced with two choices, each totally unacceptable.

No one can be satisfied with this strategic posture. One of the greatest contributions the American bishops made in writing "The Challenge of Peace" was to focus attention on the need to change our military posture. There are many differing opinions on how we might best resolve our dilemma, but at least there is a general understanding that our present position is unsatisfactory.

How did that unsatisfactory position develop? One thing is certain: over the years, as the U.S. formulated its nuclear strategy, the just-war tradition was far from the minds of the dominant strategic planners.

Immediately after World War II, the U.S. deterrent power was unquestioned. We alone had the atomic bomb, and we had demonstrated our willingness to use it. No other country could dare to challenge us directly. But when the Soviet Union developed its own thermonuclear weapons, to complement the

Soviet superiority in conventional forces, American planners were forced to devise a new policy for deterring Soviet aggression. The Soviets had already established an overwhelming conventional strength; to match it would have been prohibitively expensive. Rather than ask American taxpayers to shoulder the burden (or, as an alternative, cut down other areas of the federal budget), our government adopted a new strategic policy. The new policy came to be known as Mutually Assured Destruction—better known by the appropriate acronym, MAD.

MAD doctrine was simple. If the Soviet Union attacked the U.S., or any of its allies, the attack would be met with an immediate, massive nuclear retaliation. Admittedly that retaliation would bring on a Soviet counter-strike; it would be suicidal. But as the doctrine developed, strategic planners took comfort in the very irrationality of the doctrine. If both superpowers faced annihilation—so the argument ran—then both sides would be forced to behave responsibly, and avoid any incidents that might possibly prompt the dreaded nuclear confrontation.

By that reasoning, planners concluded that a greater threat made for a stronger deterrent: the more horrible the weapons, the better. At its height of popularity, MAD proscribed any defensive measures to protect civilians against attack. The two superpowers (in theory, again) were to confront each other naked, totally vulnerable to attack and therefore totally unwilling to risk situations that would make attack more likely. Defensive measures, according to MAD doctrine, were de-stabilizing; they might make one side less vulnerable to annihilation, and therefore less apt to avoid confrontation.

Needless to say, MAD theorists frowned on any strategies for limited nuclear war. In a complete reversal of just-war teachings, MAD taught that the two opposing sides should concentrate entirely on offensive strategies—strategies aimed at civilian targets. To aim at military targets might upset the balance; the enemy might worry that he could be robbed of his ability to inflict a crippling retaliatory blow. In a perverse way, MAD *required* the U.S. to uphold the offensive potential of the U.S.S.R. So American missiles were intentionally designed to be a bit inaccurate—inaccurate enough so that they could only be used to incinerate entire cities, not precise military targets.

The explosive power of these weapons increased steadily, so that the cost of war (in human casualties, of course) grew ever higher. MAD sought for the day when each side would have the unquestioned power to destroy the other even after absorbing a surprise first-strike attack. Then, the theory insisted, the balance of terror would be perfectly stable.

So the theory ran. But the theory was wrong. Gradually, American planners realized that the Soviet Union does not share our belief that nuclear war was unthinkable. The Kremlin was not playing the same MAD game. Moscow had embarked on an ambitious campaign of diverse weaponry and civil defense, obviously contemplating strategic nuclear superiority. Nor did the Soviet Union avoid confrontations. Instead, secure in the knowledge that Americans would not resort to nuclear overkill, they pushed forward with their policies of subversion, intimidation, and occasional outright invasion.

In Hungary, Poland, Czechoslovakia, Afghanistan —again and again the Soviet tested the Western will. In each case, it was palpably irrational for the U.S. to respond with a strategic nuclear strike, and fruitless to contemplate a conventional response against overwhelming Soviet superiority. MAD failed—or rather, worse, it worked to the Soviet Union's advantage!

Even on a theoretical plane, MAD suffered from several fatal flaws. First, the theory rewarded aggressive behavior. When one side (invariably the Soviets) acted irresponsibly, the other side had only two choices: to accept the aggressive actions calmly, or to bring on the holocaust. Similarly, MAD rewarded leaders for behaving irrationally in general. If a nation's leader seemed insane, then (his adversaries would think) he just might be wild enough to trigger a nuclear exchange. So his adversaries would go out of their way to avoid provoking him. MAD even discouraged nations from undertaking legitimate defensive actions, since those actions might prompt a counter-move, a rapid escalation, and eventually the final horrible showdown.

Perhaps it is no coincidence that MAD also failed the test of moral reasoning. Instead of a rational defense, proportioned to meet the particular threat, MAD held out one single, blood-curdling possibility: if provoked, we would touch off a holocaust. MAD failed the test of proportion and—even more miserably—the test of discrimination.

In the end, MAD also failed to satisfy the *ius ad bellum* requirement of providing some realistic hope of victory. Every defense analyst agreed that no one could win in an all-out nuclear war. And in the age-old teachings of the Catholic Church, a war that cannot be won cannot be fought.

Finally, the strategic and moral difficulties of MAD became impossible to ignore. MAD theorists lost their dominance among defense analysts. First under the Carter Administration, and then under President Reagan, the United States has begun to move away from MAD. Instead of aiming our missiles at Soviet cities, we have begun to aim more precisely for military installations. Instead of insisting that nuclear warfare would mean an all-out attack with the full force of our arsenal, we have begun to devise weapons and strategies that might limit nuclear conflict at a relatively low level. In effect, we are moving toward a posture of flexible response. That trend is bringing the U.S. back into line with the just-war tradition.

Bishops and theologians, however, are not by nature astute military or political analysts. So just as the tide was turning against MAD, the bishops suddenly discovered the moral defects of the doctrine. Just as the Pentagon had begun considering just-war criteria (admittedly under different names), some Catholics announced that the just-war tradition was outmoded.

The bishops explicitly denied the latter argument; their Pastoral Letter is an unmistakable affirmation of the just-war tradition. But "The Challenge of Peace" offers a set of strategic judgments that seem designed to uphold MAD: the blanket statement that nuclear war could not be limited; the refusal to approve of smaller, more discriminating nuclear weapons; the failure to mention defenses against nuclear war. The Pastoral follows two conflicting lines of argument. First it condemns nuclear warfare because nuclear weapons cannot be used proportionately or discriminately; then it frowns on efforts to *make* nuclear weapons proportionate and discriminating.

While the bishops pondered the question of deterrence, some analysts offered concrete strategic proposals to replace both MAD and the "flexible response" alternative. One school of thought held that we could deter our adversaries simply by possessing nuclear weapons, even if we had no intention of using them. (The problems associated with that approach are mentioned above; in brief, such a bluff would encourage the enemy to test our will, bringing us repeatedly to the brink of war.) The other school of thought proposed a more viable possibility: the U.S. could dismantle most of its nuclear arsenal, leaving just enough to deter the Soviet Union from aggression.

The strengths of that latter approach are obvious. A small nuclear arsenal would mean an end to the waste of the arms race; it would ensure the Soviet Union that we could not effectively launch a first strike, and thereby lower the level of tensions; it would be a defensive posture, more in keeping with our notions of morality in warfare. But the proposal also leads to two dangerous conclusions. First, our small deterrent force could only be used to deter Soviet aggression against the U.S. itself; no one would believe a threat to use that token nuclear arsenal in defense of another country. So we would be forced to abandon our allies. Second, and more important, the few remaining weapons could not be used against military targets, since such a small number of weapons would leave plenty of Soviet installations intact. So we would have no choice but to make the cities of Russia our targets. The "minimal" deterrent would fail the just-war test of discrimination.

Unlike MAD, or the "bluff" approach, or the minimal deterrent, a truly workable strategic defense would concentrate on meeting the most dangerous threats first. Rather than devising methods of fighting an all-out global war, we should focus on smaller conflicts first. Ideally, we should develop a defense posture that would throw up a whole series of roadblocks on the road from small incidents to all-out war. The most important element of a strategic plan is not the ability to *wage* all-out nuclear war, but the ability to *avoid* it.

Unfortunately, there are no short-cuts to national security. A military threat can only be deterred by an appropriate response; we cannot deter nuclear weapons with shotguns, nor can we stop guerrillas with thermonuclear bombs. If we hope to meet every threat with an appropriate response, we must be prepared to fight on every level of conflict. More than that; we must convince our adversaries that it is never advantageous to escalate the conflict—we would be able to meet the threat on a higher level if necessary. To devise such a defensive posture would be a painstaking process, and a horribly expensive one. But we have no choice.

The greatest danger for anyone devising a national defense is the belief that nuclear weapons provide our best defense. They do not; they are only one small part of an overall scheme. If we *really* want peace in the world, we must work toward peace on all levels. If we *really* want security, we must be prepared to make sacrifices. In the final analysis, national security is a function of moral strength. Aleksandr Solzhenitsyn made the point unforgettably clear in his Templeton Address:

> The same kind of defect, the flaw of a consciousness lacking all divine dimension, was manifested after World War II when the West yielded to the satanic temptation of the nuclear umbrella. . . . If danger should threaten us, we shall be protected by the nuclear bomb; if not,

then let the world be burned in Hell for all we care. The pitifully helpless state to which the contemporary West has sunk is in large measure due to this fatal error: the belief that the defense of peace depends not on stout hearts and steadfast men, but solely on the nuclear bomb.

V *Arms Control And The Arms Race*

Overkill—the capacity to inflict more damage than an enemy could possibly accept—is one of the most confusing elements of strategy in a nuclear age. Even a grade-school child recognizes the absurdity when he learns that the two great nuclear powers, the U.S. and the U.S.S.R., have between them enough thermonuclear firepower to kill every human being on earth several times over. What is the use of having so much excess military power? Why do we continue building more weapons, when we already have so many?

When speakers mention overkill, they generally intend to emphasize the absurdity of the arms race; they rarely provide any explanations for the phenomenon. If they considered the facts objectively, they might realize that—despite its strong symbolic value —the overkill argument is irrelevant.

If an all-out thermonuclear war ever does take place, the two superpowers will *not* kill everyone on earth. They will begin the conflict with thousands of potent weapons, but those weapons will be aimed at a relatively few targets. There are hundreds of missiles poised to strike Washington, D.C., or Moscow, no doubt. But probably none are aimed at the little towns of Saskatchewan or Tasmania. Nor will every warhead hit its target. Some missiles will be destroyed in their silos by attacking enemy missiles; some will be destroyed in flight by enemy defenses; some will destroy each other; some, in all probability, will fail to detonate when they reach the target, or will fail to fire when the fateful button is pushed.

The purpose of developing an overkill capacity, then, is not at all illogical. To protect ourselves against a surprise attack, we must have firepower sufficient to threaten enormous damage even *after* we have absorbed the first blow. We must have so many missiles that the enemy first-strike blow would not rob us of our ability to retaliate. As long as we have that ability to retaliate, our enemies will be deterred; what could they gain from a first strike?

From the moral perspective, however, the strategic justification for overkill has only secondary importance. Yes, we have the power to destroy ourselves in a nuclear war. But then we have always had the power to destroy ourselves. If we abolished nuclear weapons tomorrow, the great powers would still have enough conventional explosives and bullets and artillery shells to kill people by the millions. Even if we somehow abolished all weaponry, violent men would find ways to kill their enemies—with knives or with sticks or with their bare hands—as they always have. The point is not to make weapons less powerful, but to make it less likely that we shall use them.

Arms control is not a new vogue. We have seen numerous efforts to control weaponry, from ancient days to the present. The historical record does not give much reason for optimism. When nations go to war, they generally use whatever weapons they have at hand, regardless of the treaties they might have signed. And once men know how to design deadlier weapons, that knowledge cannot be erased from the human memory.

On a few happy occasions, warring nations have refrained from using a particular sort of deadly weapon by mutual agreement. In World War II, for instance, neither of the opposing sides used poisonous gases, although both sides had such gases in reserve. Alas, we cannot cite that restraint as evidence of a noble human nature. Each side knew that the use of poisonous gases would only cause the other side to begin using the same sort of weaponry. In effect, the strategy of deterrence worked. Neither side used gas, because each knew the other could retaliate. Arms control agreements were not a factor.

Now that the world knows the technology of nuclear weaponry, the genie cannot be squeezed back into the bottle. Even if the U.S. could reach an arms-control agreement with the U.S.S.R., several other nations would still have a nuclear capability, and several more are on the brink of developing their own. We can wish, and hope, and pray for the total abolition of nuclear weapons. But the odds against complete disarmament are imposing.

What about intermediate steps? There, too, the historical record does not encourage optimism. Since the development of nuclear weaponry, we have signed a Non-Proliferation Treaty, but we have not stopped—or even slowed—the proliferation of nuclear-armed countries. We have negotiated a treaty banning weapons in space, only to see the development of "killer" satellites, and rumors of futuristic space-based weaponry. We have signed several treaties with the Soviet Union—most notably the SALT I treaty—without slowing the arms race at all.

After a generation of arms-control negotiations between the superpowers, does anyone feel more secure? It seems unlikely. The arms-control agreements that we have negotiated make no radical changes in the arms race; the spectacular build-up of horrific weapons continues apace. In effect, the treaties define the rules of a deadly game, but the two sides continue to play that game just as aggressively. If one sort of weapon is outlawed, both superpowers simply divert their efforts into another field, and replace the banned weapon with something still more destructive.

Arms-control agreements could certainly help temper the fury of the arms race, if they were negotiated in good faith. But in thirty years of bargaining, the leaders of the Soviet Union have never bargained in good faith. The first requirement of any disarmament plan is verifiability; each side must be sure that the other is not cheating. And from the very first arms-control talks to the present day, the Soviet Union has refused all efforts to provide verification of any treaty. On the contrary, from all available indications, the Soviets have violated treaties (such as the SALT I accord) repeatedly. So American negotiators are faced with a formidable obstacle: they must somehow devise a means of assuring Soviet compliance, while the Soviet negotiators resist proposals that would enable us to detect cheating, and the Soviet military planners find new ways to cheat undetected.

No doubt the American approach to arms-control negotiations could be faulted, too. But any objective observer should recognize that our negotiators have bargained in good faith. Nothing illustrates the generosity of our approach better than the first of all efforts to control nuclear weapons: the Baruch Plan. Offered at the dawn of the nuclear age, the Baruch

Plan is the most dramatic arms-control proposal in modern history.

At the time, the United States was the only nation to own an atomic weapon. We could have conquered the world, bullying all other nations to accept our rules. Instead, we offered to give up our nuclear monopoly. Under the Baruch Plan, all our atomic weapons would have been handed over to an international body, and that body would have been entitled to inspect every nation on earth, preventing the development of any national nuclear arsenal. If the Baruch Plan had been approved by all the major powers, the arms race would never have begun; the world would have been spared the current reign of nuclear terror; the moral quagmire of deterrence would have been avoided. But the Baruch Plan was not approved. The Soviet Union vetoed it.

From the outset, the Catholic Church has argued for a solution something like the Baruch Plan: a general disarmament treaty, coupled with an international peacekeeping agency. At least in the Vatican, that argument remains unchanged. A "freeze" of the arms race, like the one endorsed by so many American bishops, would be only a temporary step, not a satisfactory solution. Only complete disarmament will end the moral horror.

How could we negotiate general disarmament, when our chief adversary resists the idea? Before attempting to answer that question, perhaps we should reflect on the nature of our conflict with the Soviet Union.

When we speak of the dangers of nuclear war, we invariably speak of a potential war with the Soviet Union. Great Britain, France, and India all have demonstrated their nuclear capacity, yet we never worry about war with those nations. We do not even fear China, although that country's government, too, is pledged to the spread of world communism. Our single, overwhelming fear is the Soviet Union. That fact seems obvious. But it warrants some attention.

We worry about Soviet power for two reasons. First, of course, because only the Soviet Union has enough military strength to threaten us. Yet even if France (for example) had the same sort of awesome strength, we would not worry so much about the threat from France. And even if the Soviet Union had much less military hardware, we would still have reason to worry. The second reason for our concern is much more serious: the Soviet Union is pledged to destroy us.

From its first days as an embryonic revolutionary movement, Soviet Communism has announced its determination to rule the world, and its willingness to use any means toward that end. The first Communist theorists justified the use of terrorism; one can still read the debates between the Bolshevik leaders (such as Lenin and Trotsky) and their socialist colleagues (such as Kautsky and Luxemburg) on that topic. When they came to power in Moscow, they made theory a reality. But the theory never changed. Lenin, Stalin, Khruschev, Brezhnev, Andropov—all have made unequivocal statements affirming their quest for world domination.

The Soviet thirst for power does not only scuttle hopes for verifiable arms-control treaties; it also threatens our security in countless other ways. As long as the Warsaw Pact menaces our NATO allies in Europe, we will have cause for concern there. As long as Soviet client states foment unrest in the world's most volatile regions, such as the Middle East and Central America, that too will worry us. As long as terrorists have Soviet support for their efforts to oust governments in undeveloped countries, we must recognize the dangers. By any one of these indirect means, the Soviet Union might cause a world-wide crisis, and bring us to the brink of nuclear war.

If we were competing with the government of France for nuclear supremacy, the prospects for disarmament would be good. But our conflict with the Soviet Union cannot be solved by a treaty. We can hope to find some common grounds for concern, and some marginal relief from the horror of the arms race. We might negotiate a treaty that would put some constraints on the spiraling growth of destructive power. The arms-control process is always worth our earnest attention; every avenue toward agreement should be explored. But as long as our two governments are so implacably opposed, the conflict will continue. We cannot realistically expect to achieve complete disarmament.

Aside from pursuing arms agreements, can we do anything else to alleviate the dangers of the arms race? Fortunately, the answer is Yes. We can constantly reassess our strategic options, and avoid danger wherever possible. We can build up our conventional forces and those of our allies, discouraging the small conventional adventures that might escalate into a larger conflagration. And if the arms race must continue, we can channel our efforts into the drive for more effective, discriminating, morally acceptable weapons systems. Each of these options is worth discussing.

First, we can reassess our global strategies. For every military commitment we undertake, we should have—or devise—an appropriate military strategy. For every threat, we must have a powerful, proportionate response. If we cannot find an effective means of honoring our commitment, then we have only two choices: to develop a new military capability or to withdraw from that commitment. Otherwise, we risk placing ourselves—and the world—in danger by relying exclusively on our nuclear weapons.

Consider, for instance, our commitments in the Middle East. President Carter pledged the United States to the defense of the oil fields in that region. Now as every strategic analyst agrees, we cannot match the Soviet Union's conventional capability there. So if for some reason the Kremlin ordered a full-scale invasion of the Arabian peninsula, we would be powerless to stop it without resorting to our nuclear arsenal. That situation is inherently unstable; it might encourage the Soviets to tempt our will. Are we really willing to risk World War III in order to save the oilfields? If the answer is Yes, is there any moral justification for such a tremendous risk? If it is No, how can we devise a proportionate defense, or must we abrogate the Carter Doctrine?

Just as we should be sure that we have a military strategy to meet every commitment, we should also be sure that all our military strategies fulfill some useful purpose in meeting our defense commitments. If we discover that some weapons serve no useful purpose, we should eliminate those weapons. At best, a useless weapons system is expensive; at worst, it might be dangerous. By maintaining a weapons system that has outlived its usefulness (or never had a strategic value), we might encourage our enemies to develop the same weapons. And perhaps *they* will find them useful.

Our most destructive thermonuclear warheads, with their millions of tons of explosive power, might constitute just such a useless military system. Those weapons were designed to incinerate whole cities in one detonation; if we sought to destroy smaller military targets, we could use more accurate weapons with much smaller explosive payloads. True, those weapons enable us to destroy Moscow. But when would it ever profit us to destroy Moscow? If such a strike were strategically useful, it would be morally unjustifiable. Yet because we have weapons capable of destroying Moscow and Leningrad, we cannot condemn the Soviets for having weapons that could obliterate New York or Los Angeles. And the Soviet Union has demonstrated its disregard for the value of human life; we can never be sure the Kremlin would *not* use those high-megaton weapons. So we live in constant fear, holding each other's citizens as hostages.

The argument over chemical and biological weapons systems illustrates the same point. Chemical and biological warfare, by their very nature, are terrorist activities, intended to victimize soldiers and civilians alike. It may be true that by holding chemical weapons in reserve, we deter the Soviet Union from using their own chemical weapons. But we could never justify *using* our chemical arsenal. So why do we retain it? Is it not possible to deter chemical weapons with other, more morally defensible weapons? Instead of matching the Soviet arms build-up step by step, we should pursue our own distinctive strengths and strategies.

In writing "The Challenge of Peace," the American bishops recognized the second avenue of approach to a more secure military posture. "It may well be," the bishops reluctantly admitted, "that some strengthening of conventional defense would be a proportionate price to pay, if this will reduce the possibility of nuclear war."

The reasoning behind the bishops' admission should be obvious. If the Soviet Union enjoys an overwhelming conventional advantage in any global theatre, then it will be tempted to try our will, and we will have no defense short of nuclear war. In Europe, where such an imbalance currently exists, the situation is unstable for three different reasons. First, a Soviet attack might precipitate our massive response, with an all-out war at the result. Second, we might renege on our commitment, plunging Western Europe into slavery. Or third, we might fight a conventional war, with the constant threat that it could escalate into a global nuclear showdown.

The bishops also recognized that a conventional military build-up would be enormously expensive—not only in terms of dollars spent:

> The need to defend against a conventional attack in Europe imposes the political and moral burden of developing adequate, alternative modes of defense to prevent reliance on nuclear weapons. Even with the best coordinated effort —hardly likely in view of contemporary political division on this question—development of an alternative defense position will still take time.

In the short run, we cannot expect disarmament. Nor can we hope to provide satisfactory non-nuclear responses to every potential threat. So for now, we must continue to maintain our nuclear deterrent. On this point, too, the bishops were clear: "Especially in the European theatre, the deterrence of a *nuclear* attack may require nuclear weapons for a time, even though their possession and deployment must be subject to rigid restrictions." [Emphasis in original.]

Still, we can take steps to ensure that our nuclear deterrent is guided by a defensible moral strategy. Toward that end, we can develop nuclear weapons that do not threaten global destruction—weapons that can be used for justifiable military purposes; weapons that can be used discriminately, and proportionately; weapons that can be controlled, so that they do not raise the spectre of inevitable escalation.

The best example of such a carefully designed nuclear weapon is the neutron warhead. Ironically, the loudest critics of nuclear overkill have been virtually unanimous in condemning this weapon (which they often, inaccurately, refer to as the "neutron bomb"). The neutron warhead was designed to have unique properties: Instead of the usual enormous explosive blast, the neutron device has a small, local blast. Instead of a huge amount of long-lasting radiation, distributed over an enormous geographical area, this specialized device would yield very concentrated radiation for a short time in a very small space. Properly used, the neutron warhead could create chaos for enemy military units, without terrorizing civilians.

Imagine this scenario: The Soviet leadership has decided to invade Western Europe. If they can break through the NATO forces in one lightning strike, the Eastern Bloc armies can march to the Atlantic in a matter of days. But without concentrating their armies on one strategic weakness, they cannot punch through the NATO defenses quickly enough. So Warsaw Pact forces gather in East Germany, creating one enormous massed army, and declare war on the governments of Western Europe. At this point, a single neutron warhead, detonated at the heart of the Soviets' staging area, would wipe out the threat of invasion, without threatening any civilians outside the staging area. In fact, as long as the threat of a neutron warhead loomed, the Soviet leaders would not dare to mass their armies in one vulnerable location. And without the opportunity to gather their forces in one phalanx of attack, the Warsaw Pact could not successfully strike through Western Europe.

Still, even as useful a weapon as the neutron warhead has its limitations. In the scenario described above, the Soviet leaders might respond to the careful use of a neutron warhead with a reckless nuclear strike against some European city. As long as the enemy has the ability to strike against our cities, we must retain some method of deterring that option as well.

Here modern technology might have something for us. The ideal defense against an all-out nuclear strike would be just that—a defense. Imagine a defensive system that would destroy nuclear warheads harmlessly, erasing the advantage of a nuclear first strike. Such a system would make escalation useless; it would eliminate any reason for a government to initiate nuclear war. So when wars did break out, they could be fought and resolved at lower, less destructive levels. The haunting fear of nuclear devastation would ease immediately.

In "The Challenge of Peace," the American bishops paid no attention to the possibility of erecting an effective defense against nuclear weapons. Their silence is puzzling, since every bishop had been given a complimentary copy of a book describing how such a system could be constructed *today*. Retired General Daniel Graham, who had been the director of the Defense Information Agency, had led a massive effort to devise what became known as the "High Frontier" project. The High Frontier concept involved a system of space-based defenses, coupled with ground-based anti-missile systems. General Graham and his team of experts insisted that the High

Frontier could destroy virtually all enemy missiles before they reached their targets, thoroughly eliminating the advantage of a first strike. Even more dramatically, they argued that the High Frontier could be put into place *today,* with existing technological devices!

Some defense analysts remained skeptical about the High Frontier claims. And certainly bishops do not have the expertise to judge between competing scientific claims. But whether or not the High Frontier concept itself is feasible, the bishops might have mentioned the possibility. Surely, if such a system could be devised, American Catholics should support it. Indeed, if *any* such possibility exists, we are morally obligated to pursue it with all our resources.

While the bishops skirted the issue, President Reagan adopted the High Frontier approach (although not the specific recommendations of General Graham's report) in a dramatic televised speech. As fate would have it, that speech took place on the very night when the bishops' drafting committee hammered out its last changes in the Pastoral Letter's third draft. Like General Graham, the President emphasized the moral superiority of a defense system that would save lives rather than risk them. On this question, the bishops' analysis was strangely incomplete.

The High Frontier concept, or anything akin to it, would revolutionize strategic thinking. President Reagan underlined the unique appeal of the idea when he pointed out that, if we develop such a system, we could immediately share it with our enemies! The system would be purely defensive, so we should have no reason to keep it secret. After all, we would be seeking to make war less profitable for everyone concerned, even ourselves.

Only one prospect could be more pleasing: The possibility that, through some miracle, we could eliminate the fundamental conflict between East and West, making wars of all kinds less likely. Miracles of that sort are rare. But every Catholic, in reciting the Nicene Creed, proclaims his faith that this earth has seen greater miracles.

VI *The Power of Prayer*

The first Catholic response to the problem of nuclear weaponry emerged in 1917. Yes, 1917: almost thirty years before Hiroshima and Nagasaki; even before the Russian Revolution.

Even among miracles, the events that took place in the little Portugese town of Fatima in 1917 stand out as spectacular. The story began when three little peasant children reported that they had seen an apparition of Mary, the mother of Jesus. Then they reported that she had promised to meet them again, and had offered a series of dramatic prophecies. At first the children's stories were disregarded; they were beaten and even jailed. But gradually, as they persisted and as curious onlookers saw them standing entranced on the site where their apparitions alleged-ly occurred, some of the local populace began to take their reports seriously.

Thus far, the story was like many other claims of apparitions: intriguing, exciting, but impossible to confirm. But then the Virgin made an extraordinary

promise to the three children. To convince the unbe-
lievers, she promised to perform a miracle—at a
specific time and place. Thousands of people—the
pious, the curious, and the skeptical all alike—came
to Fatima at the appointed time.

They were not disappointed. Arriving in Fatima
after a long steady rainfall, they waded through soggy
grounds to see the children in their trance. Then the
miracle occurred, as promised. As thousands of observers watched, the sun began to dance in the sky.
Then, while the crowd stood transfixed, the sun
plummeted directly toward the earth—toward the
drenched thousands in Fatima. At the last moment,
just before catastrophe, the sun halted its plunge, and
resumed its normal place in the sky. But the puddles
around Fatima were dry, and the people stood in dry
clothes, awestruck.

The "miracle of the sun" was the most spectacular
aspect of the Fatima story, but it was not the most
significant. The Virgin had also left the three children
with a detailed message about the world's future.
World War I would end soon, she said, but another,
more horrible war would follow during the pontifi-
cate of Pius XI. Russia (which at the time was a weak,
distant country, on the eve of the Bolshevik Revolution) would succumb to atheism, and "spread her
errors throughout the world." Eventually, the atheism springing out of Russia would force yet another
war, more horrible than either of the two preceding
it. In this third great conflagration, "entire great
nations" would be destroyed.

On some points, the Virgin gave explicit details.
World War II, she prophesied, would be presaged by
a spectacular show of unearthly light. Years later, the
only surviving one of the three Fatima children
looked out the window of the convent where she

lived as a Carmelite nun, and saw an unpredicted display of the aurora borealis. Sister Lucia immediately recognized this as the sign Mary had predicted. One month later, Hitler's troops marched into Austria, and Europe careened into war.

To date, the message of Fatima has proven accurate in every detail. Russia has emerged as a world power, to the astonishment of all Europeans. The Russian regime has exported its atheism around the world, and the Cold War has brought us to the brink of extinction. It takes very little imagination to guess which "entire great nations" Mary had in mind as the victims of the predicted Third World War.

But Mary had also offered some hope. All these tragedies could be avoided, she said, by prayer. Through the children at Fatima, she counseled a regular program of prayer and reparation, centering around the recitation of the rosary.

Since 1917, millions of Catholics all around the world have followed the program of prayer and reparation that Mary prescribed at Fatima, praying the rosary daily and praying for the conversion of Russia. Several successive popes have encouraged that practice, affirming that the message of Fatima is "worthy of belief." On the anniversary of his narrow escape from assassination, Pope John Paul II made a pilgrimage to Fatima, to offer prayers of thanksgiving and supplication for world peace.

In the United States, too, Catholic priests and bishops for years offered a steady drumbeat of spiritual advice for parishioners who feared nuclear war: Pray the rosary. Pray for peace. Pray for the forgiveness of our sins. Pray for the conversion of Russia. In churches all around the nation, the faithful remained after every Mass for a few moments, reciting three "Hail Marys" for Russia's conversion.

Somewhere along the line, these prayers after Mass disappeared from common practice. Thousands of individual Catholics continued to follow the Fatima program of prayer, but they heard less encouragement from their pastors. Gradually, the hierarchy stopped emphasizing the message of Fatima. Finally, when the bishops considered their Pastoral Letter in 1983, there was no mention of Fatima whatsoever.

Some older bishops viewed these developments with concern. During the final debate in Chicago, Cardinal John Carberry, the retired archbishop of St. Louis, offered an amendment that would have incorporated a three-sentence summary of the Fatima message into the Pastoral Letter. His amendment failed, without discussion. In fact, by a very close voice vote, the American bishops refused even to mention Fatima in the final document.

So the Pastoral Letter, which offers advice and thanks to peace activists, military officers, teachers, and politicians, says nothing about the thousands of pious Catholics who have steadfastly prayed for peace, following the guidance of an earlier generation of bishops.

Why did the bishops ignore the Fatima story? Certainly no other approach offers such a dramatic answer to the problem of war. And if the Catholic Church is silent about Fatima, who will spread the message?

Perhaps the issue should not be confined to the message of Fatima. Extraordinary though it is, the Fatima story is not a part of the Gospels; it is a "private" revelation. As the Catholic Church has taught throughout the ages, the Bible contains all the truths necessary for salvation. After the miracles of Christ's crucifixion and resurrection, no other miracles are necessary. If other miracles (such as the miracle of Fatima) encourage some people to belief, so much the better. But while these other miracles may be "worthy of belief," one can be a good, faithful, practicing Catholic without believing them. Perhaps this is why the bishops avoided invoking the Fatima message in "The Challenge of Peace": to avoid giving the impression that Catholics are required to believe in that private revelation.

Still, even without the particular witness of Fatima, the Catholic approach to war and peace is the same. Ultimately, war is caused by man's sinfulness; ultimately, peace can come only when mankind turns away from sin and embraces the peace of Christ—the peace that "surpasseth all understanding." Soon after the final Pastoral Letter was approved, Philadelphia's Cardinal Krol reminded an audience that while war has many causes, "sin is the fuse."

In the United States today, we see countless reminders that our society has not turned away from sin. We see countless crimes against God's law—crimes that call down God's judgment against us. The message that sin begets judgment is not only the message of Fatima; it is the message of the Old and New Testaments alike.

One atrocious sin merits special attention: the sin of abortion. In the United States today, thousands of unborn children are slaughtered every day. The blood of those innocent victims cries out to heaven against our country. Could nuclear war be our punishment? Anyone familiar with the history of God's people should recognize that possibility.

In "The Challenge of Peace," the bishops explicitly compare their struggle over nuclear morality with their long fight against abortion. Their Pastoral Letter, they insist, should be seen as a "pro-life" initiative, like their recommendations for legislation against abortion. But there is a crucial difference between the two crusades. The threat of nuclear war is a hypothetical threat; the slaughter of abortion is taking place right now. A nuclear war *might* cost millions of lives sometime in the future; abortion has *already* killed tens of millions of babies in America alone.

Still, the bishops' point about pro-life work is on target. If we hope to preserve human life, we must work to preserve life in all its forms. And if we hope to escape the wages of our sins, we must repent and reform. Nothing invites Divine retribution against us so much as abortion. The single best step we could take to preserve ourselves from a nuclear holocaust would be to stop the holocaust that is going on around us today.

But prayer has a power even beyond reparation for our sins. In our mortal combat with the Soviet Union, our prayers are our ultimate weapons. The leadership in the Kremlin controls an awesome apparatus of political control: a formidable army to prevent invasion; an active secret police force to squash internal opposition; a nuclear arsenal to threaten world domination. Still the Soviet giant has feet of clay. An atheist regime has no defense against spiritual revival.

Within the Soviet empire today, the signs of spiritual revival are unmistakable. Christian dissidents rise up constantly, preaching the Gospel despite the certainty of punishment. Aleksandr Solzhenitsyn is only the most visible example of a pervasive problem for the Soviet leaders: outspoken Christian leaders continue to indict the Communist system. And all over that great nation—in private homes, in the few remaining public churches, even in the labor camps of the Gulag Archipelago—Christians pray together earnestly for their deliverance. We cannot join those suffering Christians in their heroic sacrifice, but we can join with them in their prayers.

In the United States, very few people have direct control over the design of national defense strategy. We ordinary citizens are not asked to choose among strategic doctrines. We can vote for our chosen candidates, and lobby for the initiatives we support, but our political powers are limited. And even when we do support our beliefs in the political realm, we run another risk: we might be wrong! We might manage to see our best plans enacted into national policy, only to watch those strategic plans lead us into an unprecedented global destruction.

But we can rest assured of one thing. When we call upon our Lord for help, we cannot make a mistake. We might err in our own political actions; He will not. George Weigel put the point succinctly in his valuable little book *Peace and Freedom: Christian Faith, Democracy, and the Problem of War,* when in closing he wrote:

> A renewed act of faith, in God's purpose in history and our own capacities to act according to that purpose, is the most important first step that a Christian believer can take toward an effective role in work for peace. Without that first step, the work is sure to go awry. With it, the work is finally put into God's hands. God, we are sure, will not be found wanting.

Imagine how the world would look today, if the Soviet Union were converted to Christianity! Yet that is precisely the promise we have received from Mary, the Mother of our Lord. What we need to do is pray. Pray the rosary. Pray for the reparation of sins. Pray for the conversion of Russia.

The Soviet Union is a massive, powerful empire. At first glance, it might seem that we can do nothing against that power. And that first glance is accurate; *we* can do nothing. But in Christ all things are possible. If we had faith the size of a mustard seed, the Soviet Union would surely be converted. Tomorrow.

Appendix A
The Pastoral Letter: Summary

[In approving their Pastoral Letter, the American bishops also approved an official summary of the document. What follows is the full text of that summary, reprinted with permission.

Summary from *The Challenge of Peace: God's Promise and Our Response* copyright © 1983 by the United States Catholic Conference, Washington, D.C. All rights reserved. A copy of the complete text may be ordered from the Office of Publishing Services, U.S.C.C., 1312 Massachusetts Avenue, N.W., Washington, D.C. 20005.]

The Second Vatican Council opened its evaluation of modern warfare with the statement: "The whole human race faces a moment of supreme crisis in its advance toward maturity." We agree with the council's assessment; the crisis of the moment is embodied in the threat which nuclear weapons pose for the world and much that we hold dear in the world. We have seen and felt the effects of the crisis of the nuclear age in the lives of people we serve. Nuclear weaponry has drastically changed the nature of warfare, and the arms race poses a threat to human life and human civilization which is without precedent.

We write this letter from the perspective of Catholic faith. Faith does not insulate us from the daily challenges of life but intensifies our desire to address them precisely in light of the gospel which has come to us in the person of the risen Christ. Through the resources of faith and reason we desire in this letter to provide hope for people in our day and direction toward a world freed of the nuclear threat.

As Catholic bishops we write this letter as an exercise of our teaching ministry. The Catholic tradition on war and peace is a long and complex one; it stretches from the Sermon on the Mount to the statements of Pope John Paul II. We wish to explore and explain the resources of the moral-religious teaching and to apply it to specific questions of our day. In doing this we realize, and we want readers of this letter to recognize, that not all statements in this letter have the same moral authority. At times we state universally binding moral principles found in the teaching of the Church; at other times the pastoral letter makes specific applications, observations and recommendations which allow for diversity of opinion on the part of those who assess the factual data of situations differently. However, we expect

Catholics to give our moral judgments serious consideration when they are forming their own views on specific problems.

The experience of preparing this letter has manifested to us the range of strongly held opinion in the Catholic community on questions of fact and judgment concerning issues of war and peace. We urge mutual respect among individuals and groups in the Church as this letter is analyzed and discussed. Obviously, as bishops, we believe that such differences should be expressed within the framework of Catholic moral teaching. We need in the Church not only conviction and commitment but also civility and charity.

While this letter is addressed principally to the Catholic community, we want it to make a contribution to the wider public debate in our country on the dangers and dilemmas of the nuclear age. Our contribution will not be primarily technical or political, but we are convinced that there is no satisfactory answer to the human problems of the nuclear age which fails to consider the moral and religious dimensions of the questions we face.

Although we speak in our own name, as Catholic bishops of the Church in the United States, we have been conscious in the preparation of this letter of the consequences our teaching will have not only for the United States but for other nations as well. One important expression of this awareness has been the consultation we have had, by correspondence and in an important meeting held at the Vatican (January 18–19, 1983), with representatives of European bishops' conferences. This consultation with bishops of other countries, and, of course with the Holy See, has been very helpful to us.

Catholic teaching has always understood peace in

positive terms. In the words of Pope John Paul II: "Peace is not just the absence of war. . . . Like a cathedral, peace must be constructed patiently and with unshakable faith." (Coventry, England, 1982) Peace is the fruit of order. Order in human society must be shaped on the basis of respect for the transcendence of God and the unique dignity of each person, understood in terms of feedom, justice, truth and love. To avoid war in our day we must be intent on building peace in an increasingly interdependent world. In Part III of this letter we set forth a positive vision of peace and the demands such a vision makes on diplomacy, national policy, and personal choices.

While pursuing peace incessantly, it is also necessary to limit the use of force in a world comprised on nation states, faced with common problems but devoid of an adequate international political authority. Keeping the peace in the nuclear age is a moral and political imperative. In Parts I and II of this letter we set forth both the principles of Catholic teaching on war and a series of judgments, based on these principles, about concrete policies. In making these judgments we speak as moral teachers, not as technical experts.

I. Some Principles, Norms and Premises of Catholic Teaching

A. On War

1. Catholic teaching begins in every case with a presumption against war and for peaceful settlement of disputes. In exceptional cases, determined by the moral principles on the just-war tradition, some uses of force are permitted.

2. Every nation has a right and duty to defend itself against unjust aggression.

3. Offensive war of any kind is not morally justifiable.

4. It is never permitted to direct nuclear or conventional weapons to "the indiscriminate destruction of whole cities or vast areas with their populations. . . ." (*Pastoral Constitution,* #80.) The intentional killing of innocent civilians or non-combatants is always wrong.

5. Even defensive response to unjust attack can cause destruction which violates the principle of proportionality, going far beyond the limits of legitimate defense. The judgment is particularly important when assessing planned use of nuclear weapons. No defensive strategy, nuclear or conventional, which exceeds the limits of proportionality is morally permissible.

B. On Deterrence

1. "In current conditions 'deterrence' based on balance, certainly not as an end in itself but as a step on the way toward a progressive disarmament, may still be judged morally acceptable. Nonetheless, in order to ensure peace, it is indispensable not to be satisfied with this minimum which is always susceptible to the real danger of explosion." (Pope John Paul II, "Message to U.N. Special Session on Disarmament," #8, June 1982.)

2. No use of nuclear weapons which would violate the principles of discrimination or proportionality may be *intended* in a strategy of deterrence. The moral demands of Catholic teaching require resolute willingness not to intend or do moral evil even to save our own lives or the lives of those we love.

3. Deterrence is not an adequate strategy as a long-term basis for peace; it is a transitional strategy justifiable only in conjucntion with resolute determi-

nation to pursue arms control and disarmament. We are convinced that "the fundamental principle on which our present peace depends must be replaced by another, which declares that the true and solid peace of nations consists not in equality of arms but in mutual trust alone." (Pope John XXIII, *Peace on Earth*, #113.)

C. The Arms Race and Disarmament

1. The arms race is one of the greatest curses on the human race; it is to be condemned as a danger, an act of aggression against the poor, and a folly which does not provide the security it promises. (Cf: *Pastoral Constitution, #81, Statement of the Holy See to the United Nations*, 1976.)

2. Negotiations must be pursued in every reasonable form possible; they should be governed by the "demand that the arms race should cease; that the stockpiles which exist in various countries should be reduced equally and simultaneously by the parties concerned; that nuclear weapons should be banned; and that a general agreement should eventually be reached about progressive disarmament and effective method of control." (Pope John XXIII, *Peace on Earth*, #112.)

D. On Personal Conscience

1. *Military Service:* "All those who enter the military service in loyalty to their country should look upon themselves as the custodians of the security and freedom of their fellow countrymen; and when they carry out their duty properly, they are contributing to the maintenance of peace." *(Pastoral Constitution, #79.)*

2. *Conscientious Objection:* "Moreover, it seems just that laws should make humane provision for the

case of conscientious objectors who refuse to carry arms, provided they accept some other form of community service." *(Pastoral Constitution. #79.)*

3. *Non-violence:* "In this same spirit we cannot but express our admiration for all who forego the use of violence to vindicate their rights and resort to other means of defense which are available to weaker parties, provided it can be done without harm to the rights and duties of others and of the community." *(Pastoral Constitution, #78.)*

4. *Citizens and Conscience:* "Once again we deem it opportune to remind our children of their duty to take an active part in public life, and to contribute towards the attainment of the common good of the entire human family as well as to that of their own political community. . . . In other words, it is necessary that human beings, in the intimacy of their own consciences, should so live and act in their temporal lives as to create a synthesis between scientific, technical and professional elements on the one hand, and spirtual values on the other." (Pope John XXIII, *Peace on Earth,* #146, 150.)

II. Moral Principles and Policy Choices

As bishops in the United States, assessing the concrete circumstances of our society, we have made a number of observations and recommendations in the process of applying moral principles to specific policy choices.

A. On The Use of Nuclear Weapons
1. *Counter Population Use:* Under no circumstances may nuclear weapons or other instruments of mass slaughter be used for the purpose of destroying population centers or other predominantly civilian

targets. Retaliatory action which would indiscriminately and disproportionately take many wholly innocent lives, lives of people who are in no way responsible for reckless actions of their government, must also be condemned.

2. *The Initiation of Nuclear War:* We do not perceive any situation in which the deliberate initiation of nuclear war, on however restricted a scale, can be morally justified. Non-nuclear attacks by another state must be resisted by other than nuclear means. Therefore, a serious moral obligation exists to develop non-nuclear defensive strategies as rapidly as possible. In this letter we urge NATO to move rapidly toward the adoption of a "no-first-use" policy, but we recognize this will take time to implement and will require the development of an adequate alternative defense posture.

3. *Limited Nuclear War:* Our examination of the various arguments on this question makes us highly skeptical about the real meaning of "limited." One of the criteria of the just-war teaching is that there must be a reasonable hope of success in bringing about justice and peace. We must ask whether such a reasonable hope can exist once nuclear weapons have been exchanged. The burden of proof remains on those who assert that meaningful limitation is possible. In our view the first imperative is to prevent any use of nuclear weapons and we hope that leaders will resist the notion that nuclear conflict can be limited, contained or won in any traditional sense.

B. On Deterrence

In concert with the evaluation provided by Pope John Paul II, we have arrived at a strictly conditional moral acceptance of deterrence. In this letter we have outlined criteria and recommendations which indicate the meaning of conditional accpetance of deterrence policy. We cannot consider such a policy adequate as a long-term basis for peace.

C. On Promoting Peace

1. We support immediate, bilateral verifiable agreements to halt the testing, production and deployment of new nuclear weapons systems. This recommendation is not to be identified with any specific political initiative.

2. We support efforts to achieve deep cuts in the arsenals of both superpowers; efforts should concentrate first on systems which threaten the retaliatory forces of either major power.

3. We support early and successful conclusion of negotiations of a comprehensive test ban treaty.

4. We urge new efforts to prevent the spread of nuclear weapons in the world, and to control the conventional arms race, particularly the conventional arms trade.

5. We support, in an increasingly interdependent world, political and economic policies designed to protect human dignity and to promote the human rights of every person, especially the least among us. In this regard, we call for the establishment of some form of global authority adequate to the needs of the international common good.

This letter includes many judgments from the perspective of ethics, politics and strategy needed to speak concretely and correctly to the "moment of supreme crisis" identified by Vatican II. We stress again that readers should be aware, as we have been, of the distinction between our statement of moral principles and of official Church teaching and our application of these to concrete issues. We urge that special care be taken not to use passages out of context; neither should brief portions of this document be cited to support positions it does not intend to convey or which are not truly in accord with the spirit of its teaching.

In concluding this summary we respond to two key questions often asked about this pastoral letter:

Why do we address these matters fraught with such complexity, controversy and passion? We speak as pastors, not politicians. We are teachers, not technicians. We cannot avoid our responsibility to lift up the moral dimensions of choices before our world and nation. The nuclear age is an era of moral as well as physical danger. Why do we address these issues? We are simply trying to live up to the call of Jesus to be peacemakers in our own time and situation.

What are we saying? Fundamentally, we are saying that the decisions about nuclear weapons are among the most pressing moral questions of our age. While these decisions have obvious military and political aspects, they involve fundamental moral choices. In simple terms, we are saying that good ends (defending one's country, protecting freedom, etc.) cannot justify immoral means (the use of weapons which kill indiscriminately and threaten whole societies). We fear that our world and nation are headed in the wrong direction. More weapons with greater destructive potential are produced every day. More and more nations are seeking to become nuclear powers. In our quest for more and more security we fear we are actually becoming less and less secure.

In the words of our Holy Father, we need a "moral about-face." The whole world must summon the moral courage and technical means to say no to nuclear conflict; no to weapons of mass destruction; no to an arms race which robs the poor and the vulnerable; and no to the moral danger of a nuclear age which places before humankind indefensible choices of constant terror or surrender. Peacemaking is not an optional commitment. It is a requirement of our faith. We are called to be peacemakers, not by some movement of the moment, but by our Lord Jesus. The content and context of our peacemaking is set not by some political agenda or ideological program, but by the teaching of his Church.

Ultimately, this letter is intended as an expression of Christian faith, affirming the confidence we have that the risen Lord remains with us precisely in moments of crisis. It is our belief in his presence and power among us which sustain us in confronting the awesome challenge of the nuclear age. We speak from faith to provide hope for all who recognize the challenge and are working to confront it with the resources of faith and reason.

To approach the nuclear issue in faith is to recognize our absolute need for prayer: we urge and invite all to unceasing prayer for peace with justice for all people. In a spirit of prayerful hope we present this message of peace.

Appendix B
Readings For Further Study

The Bishops' Pastoral Letter generated an astonishing amount of written material, adding to an already enormous volume of literature on the morality of modern warfare. Every Catholic publication in the country provided coverage of the controversy, and most included plenty of editorial comments. The following list includes just a few of the most helpful analyses. For those interested readers who want to pursue the topic still further, there should be no difficulty finding additional reading material.

My purpose in including this reading list is twofold: first, to help readers find material that they might not otherwise have discovered; and second, to provide some balance in a debate that has often been one-sided. The books and articles listed below, therefore, all stress arguments that are underemphasized or ignored in the popular literature on this topic. I have intentionally kept this list short, by including only a few of the most important works.

Benestad, J. Brian. *The Pursuit of a Just Social Order.* Washington, Ethics & Public Policy Center, 1983. A penetrating look at how the U.S. Catholic Conference and the National Conference of Catholic Bishops put together their policy statements.

Bukovsky, Vladimir. *The Peace Movement and the Soviet Union.* New York, Orwell Press, 1982. In pamphlet form, a noted Soviet dissident explains the techniques by which the Kremlin helps to mold public opinion in the West.

Cropsey, Joseph. "The Moral Basis of International Action"; *Political Philosophy and the Issues of Politics.* Chicago, University of Chicago Press, 1977. Possibly the most cogent philosophical analysis of warfare that has appeared in our generation.

Draper, Theodore. "How Not to Think About Nuclear War"; *New York Review of Books;* July 15, 1982. Draper is certainly not a "hawk" in his approach to nuclear weapons. But his thoughtful reactions to such proposals as the nuclear freeze and the "no first use" promise are negative.

van Feldt, Elmer. "When to Turn the Other Cheek"; *Columbia,* April 1982. The influential magazine of the Knights of Columbus does not often take controversial editorial positions. This is a striking, unequivocal exception.

Graham, Daniel O. *High Frontier: A New National Strategy.* Washington, The Heritage Foundation, 1982. General Graham, the former chief of the Defense Intelligence Agency, has taken the lead in arguing for a new defense system based on space-based anti-missile systems. His ideas might signal an escape from the moral dilemma of deterrence.

Himes, Kenneth R. "The Catholic Hierarchy and Nuclear Arms"; *Forum for Social Economics,* Winter 1981/82. Written before the bishops' efforts became a popular issue, this essay provides a thorough understanding of the historical background.

Hyde, Henry *et al*. "Peace without Justice is Moral Violence." Published in pamphlet form by the National Committee of Catholic Laymen in New York 1982. An open letter to Cardinal Bernardin and the other bishops on the drafting committee, signed by 24 Catholic Congressmen, explains the legislators' desires for strong defense.

Lawler, Philip F. "The Bishops and the Bomb"; *The Heritage Lectures, #16* Washington, The Heritage Foundation, 1982. A short pamphlet, written for a general readership, and intended to help prepare American Catholics (and others) for the bishops' debate—again, written before the controversy flowered.

————, ed. *Justice and War in the Nuclear Age.* Washington, University Press of America, 1983. A collection of five essays covering different aspects of the question that the bishops confronted. This symposium represents the fullest effort by American Catholic laymen to respond to the second draft of the bishops' letter.

Lefever, Ernest, and Steven Hunt, editors. *The Apocalyptic Premise.* Washington, Ethics & Public Policy Center, 1983. A collection of essays on nuclear weapons and disarmament, this volume provides the best survey of differing responses to defense questions.

Luttwak, Edward. "How To Think About Nuclear Weapons"; *Commentary,* August 1982. The author argues, persuasively, that the disarmament movement runs tremendous moral risks, since it increases the likelihood of a major conventional war, especially in Europe.

Murray, John Courtney. *We Hold These Truths.* New York, Sheed and Ward, 1960. Unfortunately, this classic book by the Jesuit theologian who so heavily influenced the work of the Second Vatican Council is now out of print. Father Murray's analysis of nuclear weaponry—like so much of his work—is still compelling.

McArthur, Ronald. "The Challenge of Peace: A Theology of Defeat." Published in pamphlet form by the St. Joan Peace Institute in Washington. Probably the most trenchant critique of the bishops' second draft, this essay also appeared in *Catholicism in Crisis.* The author questions the theological underpinnings of that draft.

Novak, Michael. *Moral Clarity in a Nuclear Age.* Nashville, Thomas Nelson, 1983. The title essay in this collection, circulated and signed by dozens of prominent Catholics, amounted almost to a laymen's pastoral letter. Originally published in *Catholicism in Crisis,* the essay struck *National Review* editors as so important that they devoted an entire issue to it.

O'Brien, William. *The Conduct of Just and Limited War.* New York, Praeger, 1982. For someone seriously dedicated to the study of the just-war tradition, this weighty volume is *the* book; a thorough, scholarly, painstaking study of how that tradition applies today.

Ramsey, Paul. *The Just War.* Washington, University Press of America, 1983. Originally published in 1968, this scholarly work was also out of print until its recent revival. Like O'Brien, Ramsey has studied the ethical problems of warfare for years; his grasp is complete.

Schall, James V. "The Defense of Right and Civilization"; *Homiletic and Pastoral Review,* August 1982. Father Schall analyzes the teaching of recent popes on warfare and conscience, and explains the moral hazards of pacifism.

———, ed. *Out of Justice, Peace; Winning the Peace.* San Francisco, Ignatius Press, 1984. An invaluable resource! Here, in readable English translation, are the pastoral letters of the German and French Catholic bishops, along with a shorter letter by the English Catholic primate, Cardinal Hume. The reader will gain a much better understanding of *universal* Catholic teaching.

Teller, Edward. "Dangerous Myths about Nuclear Arms"; *Reader's Digest,* November 1982. The "father of the hydrogen bomb" points to several misconceptions about the weapons and the strategies on which we rely.

Weigel, George. *Peace and Freedom: Christian Faith, Democracy, and the Problem of War.* Washington, Institute on Religion and Democracy, 1983. Short (78 pp.) and readable, this book introduces the reader the Christian ethical analysis on defense issues, combining historical, theological, and political insights.

————. *The Peace Bishops and the Arms Race.* Chicago, World Without War Council, 1982. Early in the debate, Weigel assembled some of the most controversial statements by American prelates, alongside his rebuttals.